FORGOTTEN CRIMES

Suzanne E. Evans

Forgotten Crimes

The Holocaust and
People with Disabilities

With a Preface by Bengt Lindqvist

Ivan R. Dee
CHICAGO 2004

Library of Congress Cataloging-in-Publication Data:
Evans, Suzanne E.
   Forgotten crimes : the Holocaust and people with disabilities /
Suzanne E. Evans ; with a preface by Bengt Lindqvist.
      p. cm.
   Includes bibliographical references and index.
   ISBN 1-56663-565-9 (alk. paper)
   1. People with disabilities—Nazi persecution. I. Title.

D804.5.H35E93 2004
940.53'18'087—dc22

                                          2003068826

Contents

	Acknowledgments	5
	Preface by Bengt Lindqvist	9
	Introduction	15
1	The Children's Killing Program	21
2	The T4 Adult Euthanasia Program	41
3	Racial Hygiene, Nazi Doctors, and the Sterilization Law	95
4	Perpetrators and Accomplices	127
5	After the Atrocities	143
6	The Need to Remember	167
	Notes	169
	Index	183

Acknowledgments

DISABILITY RIGHTS ADVOCATES (DRA) wishes to thank the United States Department of State for its encouragement and its financial support, without which the publication of this book would not have been possible.

Disability Rights Advocates is a nonprofit corporation run by people with disabilities for people with disabilities. With headquarters in Oakland, California, and an affiliate office in Budapest, Hungary, the organization's mission is to be an advocate for people with disabilities in order to ensure their full participation in all aspects of life locally, nationally, and internationally. DRA established the Disability Holocaust Project with several objectives: (1) to shatter the silence that has surrounded the fate of people with disabilities during the Holocaust; (2) to heighten public awareness about the current desperate plight of people with disabilities; (3) to utilize the shared history of the Holocaust as a vehicle for building greater cooperation between organizations of people with disabilities; and (4) to relate pre-Holocaust Nazi concepts to pernicious contemporary attitudes and enhance awareness of the existing stigmatization of people with disabilities.

As part of the Disability Holocaust Project, DRA interviewed Holocaust survivors and historians, surveyed materials available in major archives, and analyzed all of the

6 : *Acknowledgments*

information currently available on Nazi-era atrocities committed against people with disabilities. This book represents a documentation of the horrors inflicted upon people with disabilities during the Holocaust and of the central role that the extermination and exploitation of people with disabilities played in Hitler's vision.

Disability Rights Advocates thanks the following individuals and organizations for their help with and support of the Disability Holocaust Project: Center for Independent Living, Sofia, Bulgaria; De juRe Alapitvany, Budapest, Hungary; Disabled Persons International, Winnipeg, Manitoba; Equal Ability Limited, Yorkshire, England; German Council of Centers for Self-Determined Living of Disabled People–ILS e.V., Kassel, Germany; Legal Advocacy for the Defense of People with Disabilities, Tokyo, Japan; World Institute on Disability, Oakland, California; Berkeley Center for Independent Living, Berkeley, California; California Foundation for Independent Living Centers, Sacramento, California; Computer Technologies Program, Berkeley, California; Disability Rights Education and Defense Fund, Inc., Berkeley, California; Independent Living Resource Center of San Francisco, San Francisco, California; National Federation for the Blind, Baltimore, Maryland; Jewish Deaf Community Center, Los Angeles, California; Canadian Centre on Disability Studies, Winnipeg, Canada; Avocado Press, Louisville, Kentucky; Prof. Adrianne Asch; Laura Eichhorn; Henry Enns; Dean Edwin Epstein; Rabbi A. Freehling; Prof. Henry Friedlander; Jonathan Friedman; Hugh Gregory Gallagher; Robin Gerber; Robert Gnaizda; Herbert Gunther; Prof. Hurst Hannum; Dr. Zsofia Kalman; Deborah Kaplan; Karen Kaplowitz; Patricia Kirkpatrick; Bengt Lindqvist; Prof. Paul

Longmore; Commissioner Paul Miller; Sybil Milton; Sandy O'Neill; Kapka Panayotova; Dr. Adolf Ratzka; and Harilyn Rousso, among many others.

LAURENCE W. PARADIS
Executive Director

SID WOLINSKY
Director of Litigation

SHAWNA PARKS
International Coordinator

Preface

DEHUMANIZATION of people with disabilities did not begin with the Holocaust. Nor did it end with the Nazis' defeat. While the actions of Hitler's Germany represent the most structured and far-reaching attempt to eradicate the class of people with disabilities, it reflects the treatment of disabled people throughout history. Unfortunately society has long segregated and marginalized people with disabilities, defining them as inherently nonproductive, or "useless eaters" in Nazi parlance. The labeling of people with disabilities as burdensome, noncontributing members of society then often becomes a self-fulfilling prophecy. As occurs in many forms of discrimination, the person is labeled inferior and on the basis of that label is then restricted in education, work, and life opportunities. Rather than recognize the attitudinal basis of the cycle, society then imputes these characteristics as intrinsic to the person, rather than a result of societal barriers and discrimination.

How did this process during the Nazi era become so extreme that people with disabilities became, in the eyes of the perpetrators, so unworthy of life as to become the target of categorical destruction? Holocaust scholars estimate the total death toll from the Nazi disability killings to number in the hundreds of thousands of men, women, and children.

What are the patterns of dehumanization that generate such actions?

These questions are neither historical nor academic. The propaganda used by the Nazis to stigmatize people with disabilities, the kinds of attitudes that pervaded the German medical profession, and the shameful regard of disability as abhorrent, all continue to be part of a pervasive and lasting historical legacy. They directly implicate the status of people with disabilities throughout the world today. Millions of disabled men, women, and children continue to be subjected to the same kind of isolation, exclusion, and negative stereotypes that allowed the "euthanasia" killings to occur.

Throughout the world, people with physical, sensory, and mental impairments now live largely without enforceable rights. They struggle to gain some measure of dignity in a world that is both figuratively and literally inaccessible to them. Negative attitudes create often insurmountable barriers to living independently, gaining an education or a job, and marrying and having children. Disability remains something to be hidden or fixed. At best, it becomes an object of charity or pity. Thus an analysis of the Nazi campaign against people with disabilities can inform our dialogue about contemporary issues and provide insight into the continued struggle of people with disabilities against segregation and marginalization.

The notion of "imperfect" human beings, and the unproductivity and unworthiness of people with disabilities, which played such an integral role in the Nazi programs, also lies at the root of current policy issues. They form the basis of ongoing debates involving such highly charged topics as gene testing, assisted suicide, and the rationing of health care. They creep quietly into policy debates and judicial decisions concerning access to insurance and reasonable accommodation in the workplace. The discourse on each of these topics is fraught with assumptions about the inherent worth and potential contribution of a person with a disability. In a world where the deliberate medical killing of a newborn, solely because of the infant's disability, is a matter of serious discussion as an "ethical" issue among both academics and physicians, the Nazi experience cannot be ignored or forgotten. On the contrary, important insights and warnings can and should be drawn from the Holocaust, especially when scientists, academicians, or politicians begin to make judgments about the quality of human life.

It is against the background of this history, its shameful legacy and the unavoidable questions it generates, that we can begin to understand the nightmarish reality of the Nazi disability killings. This book, which presents a detailed history of those killings, contributes immeasurably to that understanding. Disability Rights Advocates is to be commended for producing this important work, which can help all of us understand and address the persecution and neglect of people with disabilities in all its forms. *Forgotten Crimes* is an important and very timely contribution to the debate on how the full enjoyment of human rights and fundamental freedom by people, who happen to live with a disability, should be obtained. Above all the book presents convincing evidence that the human rights of persons with disabilities must be more effectively promoted, protected, and monitored.

BENGT LINDQVIST
United Nations Special Rapporteur
on Disability 1994–2002

FORGOTTEN CRIMES

Introduction

BETWEEN 1939 AND 1945 the Nazi regime systematically murdered hundreds of thousands of children and adults with disabilities as part of its so-called "euthanasia" programs. These programs were designed to eliminate all persons with disabilities who, according to Nazi racialist ideology, threatened the health and purity of the German race. The first category of people the Nazis began exterminating as part of their quest to build a master "Aryan" race was the so-called *Ausschusskinderer,* "garbage children" or "committee children," who had been born with certain supposedly hereditary disabilities. Pursuant to a decree issued by Hitler in the fall of 1939, German doctors, nurses, health officials, and midwives were required to report, in exchange for a fee, all infants and children up to the age of three who showed signs of "mental retardation" or physical deformity. Based on this information, a panel of "medical experts" decided which of those children should live or die. The children selected for death were then transferred from their homes or home institutions to a pediatric killing ward. There, shortly after their arrival, they were killed by lethal injection or placed in so-called "hunger houses" where they died slowly and painfully from malnutrition.

Ridding Germany of children born with disabilities was central to Hitler's vision of the *volkish* (people's) state. Because children represented Germany's future, Hitler considered the elimination of all mentally and physically "defective" children as a crucial step in his quest for racial purification.

Scholars disagree on how many children with disabilities were exterminated by the Nazi regime, but most agree that the number falls somewhere between 5,000 and 25,000. With the extermination of Germany's disabled children under way, Hitler was asked by Dr. Karl Brandt and Philipp Bouhler, the two men in charge of the children's killing program, to sign a decree that would expand the authority of German physicians to provide a "mercy death" to all German adults suffering from "incurable" diseases and disabilities. Shortly after Hitler signed this order in October 1939, Nazi officials began disseminating questionnaires and registration forms to all German hospitals, asylums, and institutions that cared for the chronically ill. The forms required hospital officials to report all patients who were suffering from conditions such as schizophrenia, epilepsy, paralysis, encephalitis, Huntington's disease, and severe physical deformities. Based on the information provided on these forms, Nazi doctors decided, pursuant to procedures similar to those used in the children's killing program, which patients should be killed. The men and women selected for death were transported to one of six official "euthanasia" centers, where they were gassed to death in chambers built to resemble large shower or "therapeutic inhaling" rooms. Between January 1940 and August 1941, at least 275,000 Germans with disabilities were exterminated as part of the Nazi regime's "Aktion T4" euthanasia program, so named for the location of the program's central offices at Tiergartenstrasse No. 4 in Berlin.

Despite attempts to disguise the true purpose of the T4 program, the secrecy surrounding the killings eventually broke down. Some staff members spoke of the killings while drinking in local pubs after "work"; women's hairpins turned up in urns sent to the relatives of murdered male victims; or the cause of a victim's death was listed as appendicitis when the victim's appendix had previously been removed. By the summer of 1941 concerned parents and priests throughout Germany began publicly protesting the killings. On August 3, 1941, for example, Bishop Clemens August Graf von Galen delivered a sermon to his parishioners in which he detailed everything he knew about the murders. Around the same time, grieving parents began turning to the courts or placing public notices in local newspapers about the sudden and unexpected deaths of their children who had died from mysterious ailments while under the "care" of Nazi physicians.

In response to such public criticism and concern, on August 24, 1941, Hitler ordered the immediate halt of all "mercy killings" at the six official euthanasia centers. Despite this official stop order, the Nazi regime continued exterminating people with disabilities in other regions and by other means. During this period of decentralized mass killings, sometimes referred to as the period of "wild euthanasia," Nazi doctors decided, according to their own arbitrary standards, which patients should live or die. Indiscriminate mass murder thus became part of general hospital routine as hundreds of thousands of patients with disabilities in Germany, Austria, and the occupied territories were shot, burned, frozen, starved, tortured, or poisoned to death.

Meanwhile, in the wake of Hitler's stop order, a new killing program code-named Aktion 14f13 was established in order to "weed out" from the overcrowded Nazi concentration camps all "asocial" prisoners who were too sick or disabled to work. After brief medical exams, these prisoners were transferred to nearby killing centers where they were gassed to death simply because they were unable to work.

But even before the T4 and Aktion 14f13 programs began, Nazi officials had begun killing psychiatric patients in the Prussian provinces, occupied Poland, and the former Soviet Union. Between September 29 and November 1, 1939, for example, special Einsatzgruppen squads shot 3,700 patients in asylums in the region of Bromberg, Poland. And between December 1939 and January 1940, special SS units gassed 1,558 patients from Polish asylums in specially adapted gas vans in order to make room for anticipated wartime casualties and military barracks. By 1945 as many as 750,000 people with disabilities had been murdered by the Nazi regime.

In addition to the mass slaughter, the Nazi regime also forcibly sterilized nearly a half-million Germans with disabilities pursuant to the Law for the Prevention of Offspring with Hereditary Diseases. Enacted by the German government in July 1933, the law called for the compulsory sterilization of all persons suffering from supposedly "hereditary" diseases, such as congenital feeblemindedness, schizophrenia, manic-depressive psychosis, hereditary epilepsy, Huntington's chorea, hereditary blindness, hereditary deafness, and physical deformities. Thousands of young German men and women died as a result of botched sterilization procedures and experiments involving the injection of corrosive chemicals into their reproductive tracts.

After the war, disabled victims were not recognized by government or legal authorities as persons who had been persecuted by the Nazi regime. Survivors of the euthanasia and sterilization programs received no restitution for time spent in the killing wards or for having been forcibly sterilized. Although the sterilization law had been declared invalid by the Allies, the postwar German state did not recognize sterilization under the Nazi era as racial persecution, and postwar German courts consistently held that forced sterilization under the law had followed legally proper procedures. Disabled persons challenging such rulings consistently lost their cases in court.

The appeal of a sterilized deaf person, for example, was denied in 1950 after two court-appointed physicians certified that the original finding of congenital deafness had been correct and that his sterilization was therefore legally permissible under the then-existing law. Similarly, in 1964, the appeal for restitution from another survivor who had been sterilized during the Nazi era was denied on the grounds that since he was deaf, his sterilization did not constitute Nazi persecution. To this day the German state has not fully recognized or compensated disabled persons for the atrocities committed against them by the Nazi regime. To this day, few people are aware that such atrocities happened.[1]

Although the crimes described in this book were unique to Nazi Germany, inhumane and degrading treatment of people with disabilities continues to be endemic in contemporary society. For example, Greek authorities recently ignored a concentration camp for the insane on the island of Leros until several Western European television stations made a public issue of it. And in Britain, patients in secure hospitals such as Ashworth or Rampton have been regularly abused, particularly if they are of Afro-Caribbean origin. Recent debates over the ideas of the moral philosopher Peter Singer, who maintains that "killing . . . a chimpanzee is worse than the killing of a gravely defective human" serve as a chilling reminder that the very same ideas and attitudes that led to the Holocaust are still prevalent in the world today.[2]

Remembrance of the mass slaughter of people with disabilities during the Holocaust is therefore crucial to an understanding of both (1) how and why people with disabilities continue to be marginalized in contemporary society, and (2) the attitudes and moral failures that allowed the Holocaust to happen. Until a full account of Nazi atrocities is acknowledged and remembered, we all remain at risk.

ONE

The Children's Killing Program

The right of personal freedom recedes before the duty to preserve the race. There must be no half measures. It is a half measure to let incurably sick people steadily contaminate the remaining healthy ones. This is in keeping with the humanitarianism which, to avoid hurting one individual, lets a hundred others perish. If necessary, the incurably sick will be pitilessly segregated—a barbaric measure for the unfortunate who is struck by it, but a blessing for his fellow men and posterity.

—Adolf Hitler (1923)

SOMETIME IN THE FALL of 1938, a baby was born to the Knauer family near Leipzig, Germany, a tiny village about two hundred kilometers southwest of Berlin. But what should have been a joyous occasion for the family proved to be a source of sadness and despair: the infant had been born blind and deformed. After a brief examination, Leipzig physicians diagnosed the infant as an idiot.[1]

Several days later, the baby's father met with Dr. Werner Catel, director of the Leipzig University Children's Clinic, who agreed to admit the infant to the clinic. Catel later claimed that the father had requested that the clinic's physicians kill the infant, but that he had refused to do so because "killing children was against the law." The father then reportedly appealed directly to Adolf Hitler, requesting that he bring about the child's death. After reading the appeal, Hitler ordered Karl Brandt, his personal physician, to meet with the Leipzig physicians to determine whether the information presented in the petition was accurate. "If the facts given by the father were correct," Brandt later testified, "I was to inform the physicians in [Hitler's] name that they could carry out euthanasia." Brandt was also authorized to inform the physicians that any legal proceedings that might be brought against them for killing the child would be quashed by Hitler himself. After meeting with the physicians and briefly examining the child, Brandt confirmed the original diagnosis. Shortly thereafter, one of the Leipzig physicians "euthanized" the child, thus setting the stage for what ultimately became the Nazi regime's children's killing program, in which thousands of infants and children with disabilities were brutally and systematically killed.[2]

At the Nuremberg trials, Karl Brandt described what happened to the Knauer baby:

BRANDT: The father of a deformed child approached the Führer and asked that this child or creature should be killed. Hitler turned this matter over to me and told me to go to Leipzig immediately . . . to confirm the fact on the spot. It was a child, who had been born blind, and an idiot—at least it seemed to be an idiot—and it lacked one leg and part of an arm.

QUESTION: Witness, you were speaking about the Leipzig affair, about this deformed child. What did Hitler order you to do?

BRANDT: He ordered me to talk to the physicians who were looking after the child to find out whether the statements of the father were true. If they were correct, then I was to inform the physicians in his name that they could carry out the euthanasia. The important thing was that the parents should not feel themselves incriminated at some later date as a result of this euthanasia that the parents should not have the impression that they themselves were responsible for the death of the child. I was further ordered to state that if these physicians should become involved in some legal proceedings because of this measure, these proceedings would be quashed by order of Hitler.

QUESTION: What did the doctors who were involved say?

BRANDT: The doctors were of the opinion that there was no justification for keeping such a child alive.[3]

Werner Catel later testified that he had discussed the Knauer case with the child's father but that he (Catel) left for vacation soon after the infant was admitted to the clinic. When he returned from vacation, Catel was reportedly informed that one of his subordinates, a Dr. Kohl, had given the child a lethal injection while the nurses were taking a coffee break. Although both Brandt and Catel tried to evade responsibility for the child's death, both men stressed the importance of the Knauer case to the beginning of the children's killing program.[4]

While some historians argue that the Nazi regime's euthanasia programs developed on an informal, ad hoc basis, this view conflicts with existing testimony and evidence. For example, Karl Brandt testified at Nuremberg that in 1935 Hitler told Gerhard Wagner, a prominent German physician, that "if war should break out, he would take up the euthanasia question and implement it . . . because the Führer was of the opinion that such a problem would be easier and smoother to carry out in wartime" and because "the public resistance which one would expect from the churches would not play such a prominent role amidst the events of wartime as it otherwise would." Brandt also recalled a meeting with Hitler at Obersalzberg shortly after the conclusion of the Polish campaign at which Hitler stated that he "wanted to bring about a definite solution in the euthanasia question." Hitler, Brandt recalled, "gave me general directives on how he imagined it, and the fundamentals were that insane persons who were in such a condition that they could no longer take any conscious part in life were to be given relief through death. General instructions followed."[5]

Other sources also argue against the ad hoc development of the euthanasia programs. In the summer of 1939, Hitler's physician, Theo Morel, reviewed everything that had been written since the nineteenth century on the subject of euthanasia. Morel then used those materials to write a lengthy memorandum about the need for a law authorizing the "Destruction of Life Unworthy of Life." Among other measures, Morel proposed killing people who suffered from congenital mental or physical "malformations" because such "creatures" required costly long-term care, aroused "horror" in other people, and represented the "the lowest animal level." Morel also stressed the economic savings that would result from such a law:

> 5,000 idiots costing 2,000 RMs [reichsmarks] each per annum = 100 million a year. With interest at 5% that corresponds to a capital reserve of 200 million. That should even mean something to those whose concept of figures has gone awry since the period of inflation. In addition one must separately take into account the release of domestic foodstuffs and the lessening of demand for certain imports.[6]

As Morel was preparing his memorandum, a Ministry of Justice Commission on the Reform of the Criminal Code drafted a similar law sanctioning the "mercy killing" of people suffering from incurable diseases. The law read, in part:

> Clause 1. Whoever is suffering from an incurable or terminal illness which is a major burden to him or others, can request mercy killing by a doctor, provided that it is his express wish and has the approval of a specially empowered doctor.

> Clause 2. The life of a person who because of incurable mental illness requires permanent institutionalization and is not able to sustain an independent existence, may be prematurely terminated by medical measures in a painless and covert manner.[7]

Inspired by these ideas, the Reich Committee for the Scientific Registration of Severe Hereditary Ailments issued a decree on August 18, 1939, that called for the compulsory registration of all "malformed" newborn children. In return for a small payment, German doctors and midwives were obliged to report all children under their care who had been born with Down's syndrome, microcephaly, hydroencephaly, paralysis, congenital deafness, blindness, and other physical and neurological disorders. These reports were to be returned to the Reich Committee central offices in Berlin where they would be reviewed by a panel of three "medical experts." Without seeing or examining the children whose lives were at stake, these so-called experts reviewed the registration forms, marking them with a plus sign if they believed the child should be killed, a minus sign if they believed the child should live, and a question mark in those rare borderline cases that needed further consideration. Based on these recommendations, the Reich Committee instructed local public health officials to arrange for the transfer of the children to nearby institutions that were serving as pediatric killing wards.[8] The first such wards were established in 1940 in Brandenburg-Görden, Leipzig, Niedermarsberg, Steinhof, and Eglfing-Haar. By 1943, twenty-three additional wards were located in Berlin, Hadamar, Eichberg, Hamburg, Kalmenhof, Kaufbeuren, Loben, Meseritz-Obrawalde, Stuttgart, Uchtspringe, Vienna, and other cities. Between 1939 and 1945, at least 5,000, and perhaps as many 25,000, children with disabilities were killed throughout Germany, Austria, Poland, and other occupied territories.[9]

Most of the children selected for extermination were transferred from their homes or home institutions to the killing wards in large grey buses with darkened windows. Despite the Nazi regime's attempt to keep the killings secret,

TABLE I
CHILDREN'S KILLING WARDS[10]

Institution	*Physician in charge*
Ansbach	Dr. Irene Asam-Bruckmüller
Berlin	Dr. Ernst Wentzel
Brandenburg-Görden	Dr. Hans Heinze
Eglfing-Haar (Munich)	Dr. Hermann Pfannmüller
Eichberg	Dr. Friedrich Mennecke
	Dr. Walter Eugen Schmidt
Hamburg-Langenhorn	Dr. Friedrich Knigge
Hamburg-Rothenburgsort	Dr. Wilhelm Bayer
Kalmenhof	Dr. Wilhelm Grossmann
	Dr. Mathilde Weber
	Dr. Hermann Wesse
Kaufbeuren (Bavaria)	Dr. Valentin Faltlhauser
Leipzig, University Children's Clinic	Dr. Werner Catel
Leipzig-Dösen	Dr. Mittag
Lüneburg	Dr. Baumert
Meseritz-Obrawalde (Pomerania)	Dr. Hilde Wernicke
Niedermarsberg	Dr. Theo Steinmeyer
Sachsenberg	Dr. Alfred Leu
Stadtroda	Dr. Gerhard Kloos
Stuttgart Municipal Children's Clinic	Dr. Müller-Bruckmüller
Uchtspringe	Dr. Hildegard Wesse
Vienna, Am Spiegelgrund	Dr. Erwin Jekelius
	Dr. Ernst Illing
Waldniel	Dr. Georg Reno
	Dr. Hermann Wesse
Wiesloch	Dr. Josef Artur Schreck

many people who lived near the wards knew what was happening to the children. For example, the sisters who lived and taught at the Ursberg Home for Children with Mental Handicaps had tears in their eyes as they stood by while Nazi officials herded young children onto the transport buses that would take them to Grafeneck and Hadamar. One of the sisters later recalled:

> Some of the patients hung on to the nuns for dear life. It was terrible. They felt what was happening. It was especially terrible with the girls. They knew instinctively that there was something bad going on. They cried and screamed. Even the helpers and doctors cried. It was heartbreaking.[11]

Although Nazi officials insisted that the parents of the murdered children had consented to their transfers, informed parental consent was in fact rarely obtained. When parents received official letters informing them of their children's death, many of them accused the hospitals of deliberately causing their child's death. The death notices were form letters, which typically read:

> As you have certainly already been informed your daughter, ——————— was transferred to our establishment by ministerial order. It is our painful duty to inform you that your daughter died here on ——————— of influenza, with an abscess on the lung. Unfortunately all efforts made by the medical staff to keep the patient alive proved in vain. We wish to express our sincere condolences at your loss. You will find consolation in the thought that the death of your daughter relieved her from her terrible and incurable suffering.
>
> According to instructions from the police, we were obliged to proceed immediately with the cremation of the body. This measure is intended to protect the country from the

A disabled boy seated in a chair outside Auschwitz. *(Panstwowe Muzeum at Auschwitz-Birkenau)*

spread of infectious diseases, which in time of war pose a considerable danger. The regulations must therefore be strictly adhered to.

Should you wish the urn to be sent to you—at no charge— kindly inform us and send us the written consent of the cemetery authorities. If we do not receive a reply from you within a fortnight, we shall make arrangements for the burial of the urn. Please find enclosed copies of the death certificate to be presented to the authorities. We suggest that you keep them in a safe place.

Heil Hitler[12]

These letters were signed by Nazi physicians who used pseudonyms to prevent identification or future contact with grieving parents.

After receiving their "condolence letters," some distressed parents traveled to the institutions to find out the true cause of their child's death; but they were invariably turned away by black-coated SS men who warned them never to return and to cease further inquiries. A few grief-stricken parents appealed futilely to the courts while others placed obituary notices in local papers in hopes of eliciting public outrage and attention. One such public notice read:

AFTER THE CREMATION HAD TAKEN PLACE WE RECEIVED FROM GRAFENECK THE SAD NEWS OF THE SUDDEN DEATH OF OUR BELOVED SON AND BROTHER, OSKAR REID. THE BURIAL OF THE URN WILL TAKE PLACE PRIVATELY AT X CEMETERY UPON ITS ARRIVAL.

Another read:

AFTER WEEKS OF ANXIOUS UNCERTAINTY WE RECEIVED THE SHOCKING NEWS ON SEPTEMBER 18 THAT OUR BELOVED MARLANNE DIED OF GRIPPE ON SEPTEMBER 15 AT PIRNA. NOW THAT THE URN HAS BEEN RECEIVED, THE BURIAL WILL TAKE PLACE PRIVATELY ON HOME SOIL.

Because the parents had been warned by Nazi officials not to talk publicly about their children's death, it took great courage on the part of grieving parents to take such public actions.

Despite Hitler's claim that the German people supported the "mercy killing" of "malformed children," the children's killing program was shrouded in secrecy from the beginning. Everyone involved in the program, from nurses and midwives to chemists and physicians, was required to sign loyalty oaths and vow never to speak to anyone about the killings. Those who did speak about the program were reported to the Gestapo and punished with imprisonment or death. Christian Wirth, a former Stuttgart detective who supervised the T4 euthanasia centers at Brandenburg, Bernburg, Grafeneck, Hadamar, and Hartheim, explained the "rules" of the program to a group of T4 staff members at Hartheim:

Comrades: I've called you together here today in order to inform you about the present position in the castle and what is going to happen from now on. I have been assigned the task of running the castle from now on by the Reich Chancellery. As the boss I am in charge of everything.

We must build a crematorium here, in order to burn mental patients from Austria. . . . Mental patients are a burden upon Germany and we only want healthy people. Mental patients are a burden upon the State. Certain men will be chosen to work in the crematorium. Above all else, the motto is silence or the death penalty. Whoever fails to observe this silence will end up in a concentration camp or be shot.[13]

DOCTORS OF DEATH

Most of the murders that occurred in the children's wards were carried out by young German physicians who used Luminal or morphine to kill their young patients. The medication was typically given to the children in tablet form, but if a child could not or would not swallow the pill, a lethal dose of the drug was injected, sometimes directly into the heart. Despite the Nazi regime's penchant for empty pretexts and euphemisms, the "mercy killings" of children were neither quick nor painless. Many children suffered severe cases of pneumonia or other debilitating illnesses before dying.

Some of the children's wards also had what were referred to as "hunger houses" or "starving pavilions" where infants and children with disabilities died slow and painful deaths. One such pavilion was located at Eglfing-Haar, which was headed by Dr. Hermann Pfannmüller. Described by his associates as "brutal," "temperamental," and "manic," Pfannmüller served in various state institutions before being appointed director at Eglfing-Haar. A dedicated Nazi party member, he described his young victims as "human husks" and later claimed to have letters from parents thanking him for having killed their "malformed" children.[14]

As director, Pfannmüller conducted guided tours through his institution to "educate" the public about the biological "deficiency" of his patients and to demonstrate the need for their immediate destruction. In 1946 a former German POW, Ludwig Lehner, testified about his experiences on one of Pfannmüller's tours. "During my tour," Lehner recalled, "I was eyewitness to the following events:

> After visiting a few other wards, the institution's director [Pfannmüller] led us into a children's ward. . . . About 15 to 25 cribs contained that number of children, aged approximately one to five years. In this ward Pfannmüller explicated his opinions in particular detail. I remember pretty accurately the sense of his speech, because it was, either due to cynicism or clumsiness, surprisingly frank: "For me as a National Socialist, these creatures [disabled children] obviously represent only a burden for our healthy national body. We do not kill with poison, injections, etc., because that would only provide new slanderous campaign material for the foreign press. . . . No, our method is, as you can see, much simpler and far more natural." As he spoke these words, [Pfannmüller] and a nurse from the ward pulled a child from its crib. Displaying the child like a dead rabbit, he pontificated with the air of a connoisseur and a cynical smirk something like this: "With this one, for example, it will still take two or three days." I can still clearly visualize the spectacle of this fat and smirking man with the whimpering skeleton in his fleshy hand, surrounded by other starving children. . . . The murderer then pointed out that

they did not suddenly withdraw food, but instead slowly reduced rations.[15]

Pfannmüller later responded to this accusation before the U.S. Military Tribunal without remorse or contrition: "If he [Lehner] says I tore a poor child out of its bed with my fat hands, I would say in my life I never had fat hands. I certainly never grinned at such a thing. I never laughed."[16]

A former military judge also recalled his experience with Dr. Pfannmüller. In a lecture on racial hygiene, Pfannmüller spoke of visiting a woman with a sick infant. Pfannmüller reportedly boasted that he left the child in an exposed place in order to bring about its death. He later told a state prosecutor what he had done, but taunted him by asking: "What are you going to do about it?" The lawyer said he would prosecute him for murder, to which Pfannmüller flatly replied: "Herr Staatsanwalt, before you can do that, you'll be in Dachau."[17] Between November 1940 and May 1945, at least 332 infants and children with disabilities were murdered at Eglfing-Haar while under the "care" of Dr. Hermann Pfannmüller.

But before Nazi doctors like Pfannmüller could kill their young patients, scores of German professionals and ordinary citizens had to cooperate, and they did. To begin the killing process, all the "sick" children had to be identified, marked for death, and then transferred from their homes or institutions to one of the killing wards. If a child had been previously institutionalized, the transfer was easy as local health officials simply ordered the transfer without parental consent. But because many of the children who were reported to the Reich Committee still lived at home, parents had to be persuaded to consent to the transfers. In many cases this did not pose a problem: health authorities simply deceived the parents about the real reason for the transfer, assuring them that their children would receive better treatment in the wards or perhaps even be "cured." Some parents, however, perhaps fearing the worst after hearing rumors about the true purpose of the wards, refused to relinquish their children.[18]

On September 20, 1941, the Reich Ministry of the Interior (RMdI) circulated a decree to public health officials in the federal states and Prussian provinces to help them refute objections raised by uncooperative parents. The Committee instructed the officials to explain to the parents how institutionalizing their disabled children would allow them more time to care for their "healthy" children. The decree also indicated that threats might be used if all attempts at persuasion failed. In such cases the authorities were to inform the parents that the Reich Committee "might have to investigate" their case, which could result in the revocation of parental custodial rights. Such threats usually worked, and most parents eventually relinquished their children to the Nazi physicians.[19] After the children were transferred to the wards, a Reich Committee official either ordered the attending physicians to kill the children as soon as they arrived, or requested that the physicians observe a particular child for several days and then issue a status report. If a negative status report was issued, the Reich Committee ordered the physicians to kill the child. This killing order was covertly referred to as an "authorization" to "treat" the child.[20]

Those physicians who murdered the children were rewarded with bonuses for fulfilling their "quotas." They were also awarded generous research grants and university appointments, and typically enjoyed great prestige within the Nazi regime. Although it was mostly the young physicians who killed the children, they were trained and assisted by more established physicians, like Dr. Werner Villinger, a highly respected professor of psychiatry at the University of Breslau, and Dr. Hans Heinze, a leading Nazi physician. Villinger, who was known throughout Germany for his work on the social and psychological problems of children, assured young physicians that there was nothing wrong with killing "mentally ill" children. Similarly, Heinze, a well-known German psychiatrist and chief administrator at Brandenburg-Görden, served as a "mentor" to dozens of young physicians who were eager to build their careers within the Nazi regime.[21]

For the most part, the young physicians who committed the killings had little or no formal training in pediatric medicine and no personal knowledge about the children in their "care." Nevertheless they had almost complete authority over the selection and "treatment" of their victims and complained when not enough children were being sent to them from local institutions. When that happened, some of the more ambitious physicians would drive around the countryside to the smaller hospitals and clinics and randomly select frail-looking infants and children with mild mental disabilities for transfer to the killing wards. Dr. Leonard Glassner from the Austrian institute at Valduna euphemistically referred to this procedure as "taking up a collection on the street." These young physicians routinely murdered hundreds of infants despite the fact that diagnoses of mental difficulties in infancy are highly unreliable.

Many people who lived near the killing wards knew what was happening to the children who were being sent there. Six

The children's cemetery at Hadamar. *(United States Holocaust Memorial Museum)*

months after the Hadamar killing center opened, local children routinely teased each other by screaming: "You're crazy! You'll be sent to bake in the Hadamar ovens!" And a nurse at Kalmenhof-Idstein later testified about the young children in her ward:

> Everyone talked about it, even the children talked about it. They were all afraid to go to the hospital. They were fearful that they would not come back. It was a general rumor. The children played a coffin game. We were astonished that the children understood.[22]

The Nazi regime did not limit its killing program to German children. One of the largest killing centers outside Germany was the Steinhof children's wing at the Am Spiegelgrund state hospital in Austria. Most of the wartime staff at this hospital were Nazi party members. Records later found in the hospital vault reflect the wide variety of child victims who were killed there. Children who had harelips, slight stutters, or minor deformities were routinely singled out and killed by starvation or lethal injection, while many infants were simply left outside where they froze to death.

Physicians also benefited from their participation in the killing program by conducting so-called scientific experiments on children that allowed them to further their own research agendas. Children with cerebral palsy, Down syndrome, and other neurological conditions were prime subjects for such experiments. Sometimes the children's blood and spinal fluids were drawn while they were still alive and replaced with air so that clear x-rays could be taken of their brains. And countless thousands of children with mental and physical disabilities were injected with drugs, sugar, and other chemicals to test the effects of such agents on children's organs. Generous research grants were given to physicians engaged in this kind of "scientific research."[23]

Nazi doctors also profited by selling children's organs to research labs, universities, and major corporations. Dr. Heinze, one of the original architects of the children's killing program, performed ghastly experiments on many children before killing them. After the experiments were completed, the children were "disinfected" (killed) and their organs removed and sold to university research centers. Dr. Julius Hallervorden, a renowned German neuropathologist, collected the brains of children and often bragged about the "wonderful material" he had obtained from "mental defectives" who had been killed in the wards. His collection of brains was used until 1990, when the samples were buried in a Munich cemetery. Needless to say, the consent of the murdered children's parents was never obtained for these experiments, and most parents were never informed of the true cause of their children's deaths.

After the war a conspiracy of silence and denial surrounded the Nazi regime's mass slaughter of children with disabilities. Although some physicians, like Hermann Pfannmüller, were ultimately brought to trial, hundreds of rank-and-file doctors who participated in the killings escaped justice and continued working in their positions as if nothing out of the ordinary had happened. When later confronted about their role in the killings, most doctors simply insisted they had done nothing wrong. As one scholar recently explained: "Eliminating deformed children and mental patients was not so much a phobic reaction to their presence, but the result of a culture of belief that genetic deformities were a burden on the nation."[24]

TWO

The T4 Adult
Euthanasia Program

The state organism . . . is a whole with its own
laws and rights, much like one self-contained
organism . . . which, in the interest of the welfare
of the whole, also—as we doctors know—
abandons and rejects parts or particles that have
become worthless or dangerous.

—Alfred Hoche, German psychiatrist

SOMETIME IN THE SUMMER of 1939, Adolf Hitler met
with Leonardo Conti, the Reich health leader; Martin Bormann, head of the party chancellory; and Hans Heinrich
Lammers, head of the Reich chancellory. Encouraged by the
success of the children's killing program, Hitler ordered these
men to establish a "euthanasia" program to exterminate all
adults with disabilities in Germany.[1] Lammers later testified at
trial that Hitler had said that he "regarded it as a right that
the worthless lives of seriously ill mental patients should be
got rid of." According to Lammers, Hitler "said that he
thought it right that the worthless lives of such creatures

41

should be ended, and that this would result in certain savings in terms of hospitals, doctors and nursing staff."[2]

Although Hitler initially appointed Conti to supervise the adult euthanasia program, he was quickly replaced by Philipp Bouhler, chief of Hitler's private chancellory, and Viktor Brack, a leading Nazi physician, both of whom, as noted, were already deeply involved in the children's killing program. To make this change official, and to expand the authority of other Nazi physicians who might participate, Hitler issued a secret commission in October 1939 but backdated it to September 1, 1939, to make it appear as if the euthanasia program were a necessary wartime measure. That authorization read:

> Reich Bouhler and Dr. Brandt are charged with the responsibility to extend the powers of specific doctors in such a way that, after the most careful assessment of their condition, those suffering from illnesses deemed to be incurable may be granted a mercy death.[3]

Never officially mandated by law or published in any legal gazette, this secret authorization served as the basis for the Nazi regime's T4 euthanasia program in which at least 275,000 German adults with disabilities were brutally and systemically killed.[4]

Once in charge, Bouhler and Brack met with Dr. Herbert Linden of the Reich Ministry of the Interior. Together these men began the critical task of recruiting physicians and hospital officials to help them implement the killings. At a meeting near the end of July 1940, these professionals were informed about the true purpose of the program. Bouhler explained that it was necessary to kill a certain proportion of psychiatric patients in Germany in order to make space for

Viktor Brack. *(United States Holocaust Memorial Museum, courtesy of Hedwig Wachenheimer Epstein)*

anticipated wartime casualties. He also assured all those present that no one who participated in the killings would be prosecuted for their actions. Apart from de Crinis, who claimed to be overcommitted elsewhere, every one of those present agreed to participate. The physicians then returned to their home institutions to begin the task of recruiting willing accomplices among their staff.[5]

Meanwhile, Bouhler, Conti, and Brack began searching for hospitals that could be quickly converted into killing centers. Toward that end, Linden and Brack traveled to the Inner Mission's Samaritan Foundation for Cripples at Grafeneck, an old Renaissance castle nestled high in the Swabian

Philipp Bouhler, one of the two leading organizers of the "euthanasia" program. *(United States Holocaust Memorial Museum, courtesy of Geoffrey Giles)*

Alps. After touring the facilities, Linden and Brack agreed that Grafeneck was an ideal location for a killing center. Within a few days a group of SS men began converting the institution into a human extermination center. Working through the night, they installed offices, erected high barbed-wire fences, and posted signs warning local citizens to stay away from the hospital grounds due to the danger of "pestilence" and infectious diseases. A gas chamber and crematorium were also built a few hundred yards from the castle.[6]

At the same time officials in Berlin were busy creating a wide range of covert bureaucratic agencies that would serve as front organizations for the killing program. They included the Community Patients' Transport Service Ltd., which trans-

ported disabled patients from holding asylums to extermination centers; The Reich Working Party for Mental Asylums which was responsible for registering victims and overseeing the officers who falsified death certificates; and the Community Foundation for the Care of Asylums which employed the staff that carried out the killings and acquired poison gas. The emergence of this covert bureaucracy coincided with the drafting of detailed methods whereby disabled victims would be selected and killed. In September 1939 the Reich Committee had issued a decree requesting that local governments provide, by October 15, 1939, a complete listing of all institutions in their geographical region holding "mental patients, epileptics, and the feebleminded." Each institution then received two forms. One asked for information about the asylum itself; the other requested information about patients, including their names, dates of birth, race, and citizenship. The form also asked for the names of the patients' nearest relatives, whether those relatives visited the patient on a regular basis, and the name and address of those responsible for payments. Hospital officials were also required to indicate whether the patient was a twin and whether he or she had any blood relatives who were mentally ill or insane.[7]

Attached to these forms was an instruction sheet directing that the following types of disabilities be reported:

Patients institutionalized for five years or more
Patients with the following conditions if they were also unable to do work in the institution or if they could do only routine labor:
Schizophrenia
Epilepsy

Senile disease

Therapy-resistant paralysis and other forms of syphilis

Encephalitis

Huntington's disease and other terminal neurological diseases

Every type of feeblemindedness

Patients committed as criminally insane

Patients without German citizenship

Patients not of Germanic or related blood.[8]

Based upon the information provided on these forms, a panel of junior T4 medical "experts" made recommendations as to which patients should live or die. Those recommendations were then reviewed by a panel of three senior "experts" who rendered the final decision. The names of those patients selected for death were immediately sent to T4 officials in Berlin, who compiled transport lists that were sent to officials at the home institutions, with specific instructions for preparing the patients for transfer. For example, all patients selected to be killed were to have a piece of tape with his or her name on it stuck to their backs, and all medical records and personal property were to accompany the patients during their transfer. Officials also were authorized to administer sedatives to agitated patients and were told that force might be applied to those patients who caused trouble or resisted.[9]

In most cases the transfer of patients to the killing centers was done without the knowledge or consent of the patients' relatives or guardians. In many cases relatives were informed about the transfer only after their loved one had been murdered. When relatives were finally contacted by the surrendering institution, the only information provided

The villa at Tiergartenstrasse 4, the center of operations for the "euthanasia" program—thus the code name Aktion T4. *(United States Holocaust Memorial Museum, courtesy of Landesarchiv Berlin)*

was a form letter stating that, on the order of the Reich Defense Commissioner, "the patient had been transferred to another institution . . . and that the receiving institution would contact them in due time. [The letter] also asked relatives to wait for notification and not to inquire further." "Several weeks later the relatives were informed that their loved one had arrived at the new center but that visits were strictly prohibited. Relatives were again instructed to refrain from further inquiries. About two months after receiving that letter, relatives were sent a final letter notifying them that their loved one had died, [but] that due to the danger of epidemics, the body had already been cremated "pursuant to local health regulations."[10]

THE KILLING CENTERS

The first four official euthanasia centers to go into operation were Brandenburg, Grafeneck, Hartheim, and Sonnenstein. The fifth and sixth centers were Bernburg and Hadamar. Between 1940 and 1941, at least 100,000 people with disabilities were murdered in these centers.

Grafeneck. The first "euthanasia" center to begin killing people with disabilities was Grafeneck, which operated from January 1940 to December 1940. Upon their arrival at Grafeneck, patients were told to undress, given a one-minute physical examination, then herded into a shed with walls that had been mortared and sealed. Because some patients were agitated, T4 officials tried to calm them by saying they would be given showers inside the shed. Once all the patients were inside, the doors were locked and poisonous gas was pumped in. Within five minutes all the patients were unconscious. Five minutes later, all the patients were all dead.

After airing out the shed, workers removed the corpses and sent them to the crematorium. Because the town of Munsinger was only three miles away, it did not take long for locals to make the connection between the bus transports, in which thousands of patients arrived but were never again seen, and the dark plumes of smoke that polluted the countryside with the smell of burning flesh. By July 1940 the killing center at Grafeneck had aroused such concern in nearby Württemberg that Bishop Wurm, head of the Lutheran church in the province, sent a letter to Minister of the Interior Wilhelm Frick:

> For some months past, insane, feeble-minded, and epileptic patients have been transferred on the orders of the Reich Defense Council. Their relatives are informed a few weeks later that the patient concerned has died of an illness, and that, owing to the danger of infection, the body had to be cremated. Several hundred patients from institutions in Württemberg alone must have met their death in this way, among them war-wounded of the Great War. The manner of action, particularly of deceptions that occur, is already sharply criticized. Everybody is convinced that the causes of deaths which are officially published are selected at random. When, to crown everything, regret is expressed in the obituary notice that all endeavors to preserve the patient's life were in vain, this is felt to be a mockery. The air of mystery gives rise to the thought that something is happening that is contrary to justice and cannot therefore be defended by the government. It also appears very little care was taken in

the selection of the patients destined for annihilation. The selections were not limited to insane persons, but included also persons capable of work, especially epileptics.[11]

"What conclusions," Wurm continued, "will the younger generation draw when it realizes that human life is no longer sacred to the state? There can be no stopping once one starts down this decline. God does not permit people to mock Him. Either the National Socialist state must recognize the limits which God has laid down, or it will favor a moral decline and carry the state down with it."[12]

Frick did not respond to the letter, so Wurm wrote to him again on September 5, 1940:

Dear Reich Minister: On July 19th I sent you a letter about the systematic extermination of lunatics, feeble-minded and epileptic persons. Since then this practice has reached tremendous proportions: recently the inmates of old-age homes have also been included. The basis for this practice seems to be that in an efficient nation there should be no room for weak and frail people. It is evident from the many reports which we are receiving that the people's feelings are being badly hurt by the measures ordered and that the feeling of legal insecurity is spreading which is regrettable from the point of view of national and state interest.[13]

Frick must have forwarded these letters to Heinrich Himmler, SS leader and chief of the German police, because in early December Himmler sent the following memo to Viktor Brack:

Dear Brack: I hear there is great excitement on the Alb because of the Grafeneck Institution. The population recog-

*Hartl
ter to
in Au:
was u
over t
conve
the fi
cility

A
ters w
the ki
fence
a fen
ing pa
dressi
locate
show
perso
Hartl
so ful
corps
them

1
meml
youn;
them
were
two c
burni
haule
the L*

nizes the gray automobiles of the SS and think they know what is going on at the constantly smoking crematory. What happens there is a secret and yet is no longer one. Thus the worst feeling has arisen there, and in my opinion there remains only one thing, to discontinue the use of the institution in this place and in any event disseminate information in a clever and sensible manner by showing motion pictures on the subject of inherited and mental diseases in just that locality. May I ask for a report as to how the difficult problem is solved?[14]

Shortly after Himmler wrote this letter, Grafeneck ceased operating as a killing center, but not before tens of thousands of people with disabilities had been murdered in its gas chamber.

Brandenburg. Like Grafeneck, the Brandenburg T4 killing center was established in January 1940. Its first director was Adolf Gustav Kaufmann, who was chief of the T4's Inspector's Office. He supervised the initial work to create the human slaughterhouse. Once the renovations were complete, Kaufmann turned over the institution to Irmfried Eberl, who served as Brandenburg's physician-in-charge. As Henry Friedlander explains, "the actual killing [facilities at Brandenburg were] located on the ground floor, [as were] a number of rooms [that] were used for receiving" and examining the patients. "The Brandenburg gas chamber was disguised as a shower room," but because showerheads were not immediately installed, "patients were told they were entering an 'inhalation room' for therapeutic reasons. Only later were showerheads added." Not far from the gas chamber was the crematorium, consisting of "two mobile ovens attached to

the ch
this ta
foul-s
1940,
The r
cated
driver

V
helm
were
ered i
to wa
of mo
at Bra

I
s
(
a
li
s
t
t
c
r
t
.
t
t
c
t

Hartheim Castle, near Linz. *(United States Holocaust Memorial Museum, courtesy of Andras Tsagatakis)*

The leading T4 official at Hartheim was Christian Wirth, a former Stuttgart detective. After leaving Hartheim, Wirth became commandant of Belzec and then inspector of the camps at Treblinka, Chelmno, and Sobibor. Wirth was described by his associates as one of the cruelest Nazi murderers involved in the T4 program. Franz Stangl, who participated in the T4 killings before becoming commandant of Treblinka, said this of Wirth:

> Wirth was a gross and florid man. My heart sank when I met him. He stayed at Hartheim for several days that time and often came back. Whenever he was there he addressed us daily at lunch. And here it was again this awful verbal crudity: when he spoke about the necessity for this

euthanasia operation he was not speaking in humane or scientific terms. . . . He spoke about doing away with useless mouths, and that sentimental slobber about such people made him "puke." The extent to which Wirth was loathed even by his own men is reflected in the testimony of SS-Scharfuhrer Suchomel, who served under him: "From my activity in the camps of Treblinka and Sobibor, I remember that Wirth in brutality, meanness, and ruthlessness could not be surpassed. We therefore called him "Christian the Terrible" or "the wild Christian.""[20]

Wirth's name comes up again in Stangl's testimony about his days in Treblinka:

> To tell the truth, one did become used to it . . . they [the victims] were cargo. I think it started the day I first saw the Totenlager [extermination area] in Treblinka. I remember Wirth standing there, next to the pits full of black-blue corpses. It had nothing to do with humanity—it could not have. It was a mass—a mass of rotting flesh. Wirth said: "What shall we do with this garbage?"[21]

In addition to serving as an extermination center, Hartheim also provided "scientific" testing grounds for the perfection of mass murder techniques. Young Nazi doctors experimented with various mixtures of gases in order to find the most deadly combinations. During these experiments, physicians with stopwatches observed the dying patients through the "viewing window" in the chamber door, and the length of the death process was timed to one-tenth of a

Christian Wirth, a former detective, worked at several killing centers before becoming commandant of Belzec. *(United States Holocaust Memorial Museum, courtesy of Bundesarchiv)*

second. Slow-motion pictures were also taken for later study by psychiatric experts at T4 headquarters in Berlin. The brains of many victims were removed during autopsies, then sold to the highest bidders.[22]

The total number of people with disabilities killed at Hartheim is difficult to estimate. But at the Dachau trial in 1947, testimony indicated that three hundred to four hundred "useless eaters" were exterminated in the Hartheim gas chambers *every day*. After Hitler issued his stop order that put an end to the official T4 program, Hartheim became an extermination center for Jews, Roma Gypsies, and other targets of Nazi atrocities.[23]

Sonnenstein. A fourth T4 killing center opened in June 1940 in the Sonnenstein Institution in the city of Prina, near Dresden. This center was the only one of the six that did not occupy the entire hospital, making secrecy impossible. When patients arrived at Sonnenstein, they were told to undress. They were then examined by a physician and sent to the gas chamber in groups of about seventy-five. After the patients were dead, their corpses were pried apart and dragged to the crematorium. It was at this point that Nazi officials began looting and mutilating the corpses. Some corpses, which had black marks stamped on their backs, underwent autopsies. These autopsies both provided young physicians with specialized training and allowed T4 officials to harvest bodily organs that were sold to research labs and universities for "scientific" study. Patients with valuable dental work had also been specially marked. The stokers usually pried the victims' gold fillings from their mouths, then sent the fillings to the

T4 central office in Berlin. The gold was collected by the German Reich, but T4 officials received bonuses and credit for their budgets based upon the amount of gold they extracted from their victims' bodies.[24]

As Friedlander explains, the disposal of corpses proved to be technically more difficult than the killings. Sometimes the corpses were piled so high that the stokers had to work though the night to cremate all the patients that had been murdered the previous day. The workload was so great at times that corpses began decomposing before they could be cremated. After cremation the stokers used a mill to grind down those bones that remained after the fire. Some of the ashes were then placed into urns for burial. When relatives of the murdered patients were notified about their loved one's death several months later, they were told they could obtain an urn of their beloved's ashes. The stokers simply shoveled ashes from a huge pile and filled the urns in a random, assembly-line manner, so the ashes did not necessarily belong to the person whose name appeared on the urn.[25]

Because of the need for secrecy, every victim's death certificate had to be falsified. To maintain an appearance of credibility, physicians were instructed to take great care in assigning causes of death that were consistent with the patients' prior physical and mental state. The doctors matched the age, sex, and physical condition of each patient to one of at least sixty-one false causes of death. In each case "the etiology, symptoms, treatment and possible complications were precisely recorded." Every example on the list of false causes of death included the benefits and drawbacks of using that particular cause of death. Some of the examples read as follows:

Meningitis
Abscesses on the brain are relatively rare as such and require a long period to develop, so that this illness can only be considered by us in a few very exceptional cases. It is useful if any of these symptoms are already evident, such as a discharge of pus from the ears, noses or sinuses. . . . Every age group can be affected by this illness.

Pneumonia
Pneumonia is an ideal cause of death for our action, because the population at large regards it as a critical illness which means therefore that its life-endangering character will be plausible. . . . Pneumonia can occur in every age-group and in both sexes. In the case of young and fit individuals, one simply has to calculate a somewhat longer duration than in the case of elderly and frail patients.

Strokes
This cause of death is especially suitable in the case of older people, of at least forty or more years of age; in the case of young people it is so rare that one should not choose it. As a cause of death it is particularly suitable because it is so sudden, has no particular contributory symptoms, and results in the patient dying a relatively painless death. This cause of death always seems reasonable to relatives, and they like to believe in it. It is also credible that the patient has died without any prior symptoms.[26]

Maintaining this medical cover-up required an extensive bureaucracy of deception. At each killing center there was a Special Registry Office, employing dozens of staff members whose primary duty was to determine a suitable date of death for each patient. Using "timecards" and "death files," these staff members could prevent the recording of large numbers of deaths at the same time, which would surely have aroused suspicion.

After a date and cause of death was assigned to each victim, a series of form letters were mailed to the relatives of the murdered patients. The first letter simply notified the relative or guardian that the patient had safely arrived from the surrendering institution. Because most patients were killed the day of their arrival, they were already dead when the notification of their safe arrival at the institution was mailed. After the first letter was sent, the killing center staff waited up to two months before sending notification that the patient had died. The opening paragraph of this "condolence letter" informed the relatives about the patient's "sudden and unexpected" death. The second paragraph would always contain elements of the official propaganda in favor of euthanasia, such as stating that the patient was suffering and that the family was now relieved of the burden of having to care for them. The letters typically included phrases such as "we offer our heartfelt condolences for your loss, and beg you to find comfort in the thought that your son was released from a severe and incurable disease."[27]

One such "condolence letter" read as follows:

> Landes-Heil-und Pflegeanstalt
> 25 March 1941

Dear Frau U.,
On 13 March 1941 your husband Ernst U. was transferred to our asylum, in accordance with a ministerial decree issued on the instructions of the Reich Defense Commissar. This measure took place in the context of the current

military situation. We regret to have to inform you that the patient died suddenly and unexpectedly of acute meningitis on 24 March 1941. Since your husband suffered from a grave and incurable mental illness, you must regard his death as a form of deliverance.

Since our asylum is merely to be regarded as a transit asylum, a stay here being partly for the purpose of establishing whether any of the patients are carrying infectious diseases (which experience teaches us is often the case with mental patients), the health police responsible for the prevention of contagious diseases ordered the immediate cremation of the body. Your consent is superfluous in cases like this. If you would like to inter the urn with the remains in a cemetery or family burial plot near your home, then please let us have proof of the acquisition or possession of the burial place within fourteen days. We will then send the urn free of charge to the cemetery concerned. Otherwise we will bury the urn elsewhere. The clothes of the deceased had to be disinfected for the reasons given earlier. They were badly damaged during disinfection. When you have given us proof of being the legitimate heir we will be happy to send you the clothes and effects, the latter consisting of a wedding ring. If we do not receive proof of inheritance within fourteen days, we will give the clothing to the poor and needy patients in the asylum. We ask you to inform other relatives of the patient since we possess no other addresses. We enclose two death certificates which you should keep safe for presentation to the authorities.

Heil Hitler,
Dr. Fleck [the alias used by Dr. Gunther Hennecke][28]

The euthanasia center at Sonnenstein closed in August 1941. By then, Nazi doctors there had murdered at least ten thousand adults with disabilities.

Bernburg and Hadamar. The fifth and sixth T4 killing centers were Bernburg and Hadamar. Bernburg replaced Brandenburg in September 1940. Before 1940 the institution had served as the Bernberg State Hospital and Nursing Home. The Hadamar killing center, which opened in January 1941, replaced the Grafeneck institution. Records indicate that at least 40,000, and perhaps as many as 400,000, people with disabilities were killed at Hadamar before it was liberated by American troops in April 1945. The Hadamar Institution was also originally a state hospital and nursing home and had been in operation since the mid-nineteenth century. After it was converted into a killing center, thousands of adults with disabilities were killed there by mass gassings or executions. Most of the children who were sent there were killed by lethal injection.[29]

When patients arrived at Hadamar, they were met by a staff member who led them to a reception room where they were told to undress. The patients were then weighed and taken, one by one, into a small room where a physician briefly examined them. Each patient was assigned a number, which was either stamped onto their bodies or attached to their backs with tape. The patients then entered another room to be photographed from the front, side, and back. These pictures completed the patient's final record and were used by German physicians to demonstrate the "physical inferiority" of their murdered patients.[30]

Once the registration process was complete, the patients were assembled in a holding room and led into the

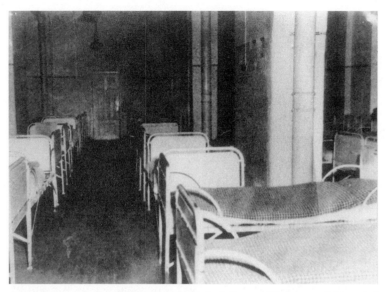

A hospital ward at Hadamar. *(United States Holocaust Memorial Museum)*

gas chamber. Most of the patients were prepared for the "showers" because, while they were undressing, the nurses told them they would be bathed. Most patients accepted the nurses' explanation and entered the chamber willingly. When all the patients were in the chamber, a staff member closed the door and hermetically sealed the ventilation shafts. A chemist in the adjacent room then opened the valve of a compressed gas canister and lethal gas began pouring into the chamber. Within ten minutes all the patients were dead.[31]

One T4 staff member later recalled that the killing of the ten thousandth victim at Hadamar during the summer of 1941 had been celebrated as a happy milestone. The entire hospital staff attended the celebration where beer and wine were served. After the "cocktail hour," the staff proceeded to the basement to witness the burning of the ten thousandth victim. The naked corpse was decorated with fresh flowers arranged attractively around flags bearing the Nazi swastika. One of the doctors delivered an encouraging speech to the participants about the importance of their work at Hadamar. The body was then thrust into a furnace, at which point the staff burst into wild applause. Several staff members performed a mock eulogy of the victim while the others danced to the sound of a local polka band.[32]

> One staff member later recalled the events of the evening: There on a stretcher lay a naked male corpse with a huge hydrocephalic head. . . . I am certain that it was a real dead person and not a paper corpse. The dead person was put by the cremation personnel on a sort of trough and shoved into the cremation oven whereupon [the administrator], who had made himself look like a sort of minister, held a [mock] burial sermon.[33]

Another participant reported that the celebration lasted until late into the night and degenerated into a drunken procession through the institution grounds.[34]

As was the case at the other killing centers, signs on the road leading to Hadamar prohibited local inhabitants from entering. Nevertheless the locals quickly figured out what was happening to the patients who had been sent there. Not long after the first busload of patients had been killed at Hadamar, local children began referring to the transport buses as "murder boxes" and "killing crates." And children often teased each other by saying: "You're an idiot! You'll be sent to bake in Hadamar." But it was not until August 1941,

The Hadamar Institution. *(United States Holocaust Memorial Museum)*

when Bishop Clemens August Graf von Galen condemned the killings, that any adults dared to speak publicly about what was happening at Hadamar.

"Citizens of Munster," the bishop addressed his parishioners:

> If you establish and apply the principle that you can kill "unproductive" human beings, then woe betide us all when we become old and frail! If one is allowed to kill unproductive people, then woe betide the invalids who have used up, sacrificed and lost their health and strength in the productive process. If one is allowed to remove one's unproductive fellow human beings, then woe betide loyal soldiers who return to the homeland seriously disabled, as cripples, as invalids. . . . Woe to mankind, woe to our German

nation, if God's holy commandment "Thou shalt not kill!" which God proclaimed in Mount Sinai amidst thunder and lightning, which God our creator inscribed in the conscience of mankind from the very beginning, is not only broken, but if this transgression is actually tolerated, and permitted to go unpunished.[35]

Tens days after von Galen delivered this sermon, the Bishop of Limburg sent a letter to the Reich Minister of Justice:

I consider it my duty to present the following as a concrete illustration of destruction of so-called "useless life." About 8 Kilometers from Limburg in the little town of Hadamar, on a hill overlooking the town, there is an institution which had formerly served various purposes and of late had been used as a nursing home. This institution was renovated and furnished as a place in which, by consensus of opinion, the above mentioned Euthanasia has been systematically practiced for months—approximately since February 1941. This fact is, of course, known beyond the administrative district of Wiesbaden. . . . Several times a week buses arrive in Hadamar with a considerable number of such victims. School children of the vicinity know this vehicle and say "here comes the murder-box again." After the arrival of the vehicle, the citizens of Hadamar watch the smoke rise out of the chimney. . . . All God-fearing men consider this destruction of helpless beings a crass injustice. . . . Officials of the State Police, it is said, are trying to suppress discussions of the Hadamar occurrences by means of severe threats . . . I beg you most humbly, Herr Reich Minister, in the sense of the report of the Episcopate of 16 July of this year, to prevent further transgressions of the Fifth Commandment of God.[36]

Nazi officials initially responded to these public complaints by punishing the protesters. Pastor Paul Gerhard Braune, director of the Hoffnungstaler hospital and vice president of the Central Committee of the Protestant Home Mission, was arrested by the Gestapo shortly after he complained that the "mass methods used so far have quite evidently taken in many people, who are to a considerable degree of sound mind." Other religious leaders who protested the killings, such as Bernard Lichtenberg of St. Hedwig's Cathedral in Berlin, were rounded up and arrested.[37] But by the late summer of 1941, the killings had caused so much public unrest that Herr Schlegelberger, secretary of state in the Reich Ministry of Justice, warned Hitler that "confidence in the German medical profession, especially the administration of mental institutions, is being severely shaken."[38] Even Heinrich Himmler, referring to the killings at Grafeneck, acknowledged the problem. "The public temper is ugly," Himmler warned Hitler, "and in my opinion there remains only one option: discontinue the operation of the institution in this locality."[39] Not willing to undermine public support for the Nazi regime, Hitler ordered Karl Brandt to "stall" the T4 euthanasia program on August 24, 1941. But by then, at least 70,000 and perhaps as many as 250,000 people with disabilities had been murdered in the six T4 killing centers.

"WILD EUTHANASIA"

Although the Nazi regime's T4 euthanasia program officially ended on August 24, 1941, Hitler's stop order applied only to the six official killing centers and to the use of poison gas.

The mass slaughter of people with disabilities thus continued in other regions and by other means. This period of decentralized medical killing, referred to as "wild euthanasia," continued until 1945.[40]

The experimentation on people with disabilities done by Arthur Nebe, chief of the Reich Office of the Detective Forces, in Belarus in 1941 was indicative of the kinds of atrocities that were being committed throughout the region during the period of "wild euthanasia." Nebe first conducted an "experiment" in Minsk, with the assistance of Albert Widmann and Widmann's assistant, Hans Schmidt. This experiment, which was part of an effort to identify efficient ways to kill large groups of people, entailed locking approximately ten psychiatric patients in a large box and blowing the box up with dynamite. The explosion caused body parts to fly over a large distance; some stuck in the limbs of trees. Since so much cleanup was required after this experiment, Nebe and his associates decided that dynamite was not a desirable method of mass slaughter.[41]

The second experiment of Nebe and Widmann, conducted in the nearby town of Mogilev, tested a different strategy to murder people with disabilities. Nebe locked a group of patients with disabilities in a sealed room and piped exhaust fumes from a truck into the room with a hose. The patients were dead within minutes; the perpetrators, relieved that they did not have to clean up body parts, deemed this experiment a success and further developed this method of killing.[42]

Another example of the horrors that occurred during the period of wild euthanasia was described in a postwar trial by Dr. Wilhelm Gustav Schueppe. Between September 1941 and March 1942, Schueppe was assigned by T4 officials to the Kiev Pathological Institute, where he participated in a special program which he described as "the destruction of life un-worthy of life." The ultimate goal of this "special operation" was to liquidate the entire disabled population in the Soviet Union. Schueppe later estimated that during his service at the Kiev Institute, more than 100,000 patients were killed.[43]

The fate of people with disabilities in the Prussian provinces was equally grim. In early 1940, large numbers of disabled patients began arriving at the Meseritz-Obrawalde hospital in Pomerania. There the staff selected for killing all those patients who were "deaf-mute, ill, obstructive, undisci-plined," or unable to work. The exact number of people killed there will never be known because only a portion of the records survived, but even the most conservative estimates claim that nearly seven thousand patients were killed by Meseritz physicians during the wild euthanasia period. A less conservative but perhaps more accurate estimate by the post-war German judiciary placed the number of disabled patients killed at more than ten thousand. The mass slaughter also continued in other occupied countries. In Bohemia and Moravia, for example, German patients were transferred to the Sudetentland for sterilization and extermination. And the removal of more than seven hundred ethnic Germans from the independent puppet state of Slovakia fostered rumors that they had been "turned into soap."[44]

"HUNGER HOUSES" AND "STARVING PAVILIONS"

After Hitler issued his stop order, hospital physicians and di-rectors found ways other than mass gassing to dispose of their "worthless" patients. On November 17, 1942, the directors of several Bavarian asylums gathered for a conference chaired by Dr. Walter Schultz, who declared that since the centrally organized mass gassings of people with disabilities had been stopped, it was time for "the asylums to do something themselves." Also taking part in the discussion was Dr. Valentin Faltlhauser of Kaufbeuren-Irsee, who recommended that the asylums starve their patients to death. To accomplish this, Faltlhauser suggested two alternative diets—one for those patients who were able to work, another for those who were not. The latter group of patients, Faltlhauser suggested, should receive no more than fifty grams of boiled vegetables a day.[45]

Most of the doctors attending the conference agreed that "starvation diets" were a helpful idea, and on November 30, 1942, Schultz informed governmental officials of the introduction of "differential diets" in the Bavarian asylums:

> With regard to wartime food supplies and the state of health of those asylums patients who work, we can no longer justify the fact that all inmates of asylums are receiving the same rations, without regard on the one hand to whether they perform productive labor or are in therapy, or on the other hand to whether they are simply being kept in the asylum without performing any labor worthy of the name. It is therefore decreed, with immediate effect, that those inmates of asylums who do productive work or who are receiving therapy, and in addition, children who are capable of being educated, war casualties and those suffering from geriatric psychosis, shall be better

fed—in both quantitative and qualitative respects—than the remaining inmates.[46]

At Eglfing-Haar, where Dr. Hermann Pfannmüller was in charge, patients subjected to these special diets were grouped in two houses that were referred to as "hunger houses." The starvation diets were ruthlessly enforced by Pfannmüller, who reportedly visited the asylum kitchen three or four times a week to make sure that the food did not contain "illicit" protein supplements. Between 1943 and 1945, at least 429 patients died from starvation in the two hunger houses at Eglfing-Haar.[47]

Enforced starvation was also practiced at Hadamar and many other German hospitals and asylums. But because starvation was a relatively slow process, the killing schedule was sometimes accelerated by lethal injections.[48]

THE ROLE OF THE SS IN "EUTHANASIA" KILLINGS

Although the SS played a secondary role in the official T4 program, Himmler and his SS men had been routinely and systematically murdering Europeans with disabilities as early as October 1939. To help streamline the mass killing process, special SS units were created. On July 3, 1939, SS-Brigade-fuhrere Schafer ordered the establishment of a special SS unit, known as the Wachsturmbann Eimann (or the Eimann Battalion), named for its leader, Kurt Eimann. One of the battalion's first assignments was to execute all the "mental defectives" from several Pomeranian asylums as part of a deal to empty the asylums to make room for military barracks and anticipated wartime casualties.[49]

To empty the asylums, Eimann and his men drugged the patients, then put them in handcuffs and straitjackets and transported them by train to Danzig-Neustadt. Once there, the patients were loaded into trucks and driven into the forest where, one by one, they were led to the edge of a large pit and shot in the back of the head. Although no one knows exactly how many patients the Eimann battalion murdered, their own report, dated January 1941, states that more than three thousand patients were killed in this manner.[50]

Between May 21 and June 8, 1941, an additional 1,558 psychiatric patients were murdered by another special SS unit, known as the Lange Commando, led by Herbert Lange.[51] Unlike Eimann's men, who shot their victims, the Lange Commando men killed their victims by mass gassing. To disguise the true purpose of their missions, Lange and his men drove large trucks, some of which had the name Kaisers Kaffee Geschäft (Kaiser Coffee Company) painted on the side as a decoy, to local hospitals. There they gathered a large number of patients, loaded them into the trucks, and gassed them to death while driving away. Lange's men then buried the bodies in mass graves in the countryside and returned to the hospitals for another "trip."[52]

The mass extermination of people with disabilities proceeded even more systematically in occupied Poland. Between 1939 and 1944 the SS and other Nazi officials killed at least 12,850 Polish psychiatric patients. In October 1939, SS units began "emptying" the Owinka asylum in the province of Poznan. The first group of patients to be murdered were the criminally insane, who were loaded onto trucks with their hands tied behind their backs, then driven into the forest by several SS guards who were armed with guns and shovels. Each time the guards returned from their "trip" the trucks were empty and the shovels were covered with dirt and blood. After all the adult patients at the asylum had been killed, the SS men began murdering the children. By November 1939 the asylum was empty. In all, nearly one thousand children and adults with mental disabilities had been brutally killed.[53]

But the mass slaughter in Poland and the other regions could be seen as small compared to the massive killing operations that began when Germany invaded the Soviet Union in June 1941. Killing Soviet civilians with disabilities was a job assigned to certain Einsatzgruppen squads, the Sipo and the SD. Although the central mission of the Einsatzgruppen was killing Jews and Soviet prisoners of war, they did not exclude the disabled community from their murderous sprees. The fate of Soviet civilian Vladimir Romanenko, who initially had been arrested as a spy, exemplifies the treatment of people with disabilities. Although Romanenko was ultimately cleared of espionage charges, he was executed by the Nazis because he was "retarded." The decision to kill him was explained as follows: "As the Romanenko case involved a retarded person, who admitted that he had already been committed to a mental hospital three times, he was executed on Sept. 9, 1941, for reasons of hereditary health." Romanenko was just one of more than 100,000 people with disabilities who were executed in the former Soviet Union during the Nazi era.[54]

In addition to these killings, the SS was also involved in the expansion of the T4 program to the concentration camps under a program code-named Aktion 14f13.

AKTION 14F13

In early 1941, Heinrich Himmler asked Philipp Bouhler about the possibility of using some of the T4 facilities to rid the concentration camps of prisoners who were "seriously ill." Shortly thereafter a new killing program, code-named Aktion 14f13, began. (The program was named for the abbreviation used for the inspectorate of the concentration camps, followed by the code used to describe the death of a "sick inmate.") Among the markings used to identify "seriously ill" prisoners was an armband inscribed with the German word "Blöd," which indicated that the prisoner was "feebleminded." Similarly, deaf prisoners were forced to wear small metal pins in the shape of an inverted red triangle, inscribed with the word *Taubstummen*, meaning "deaf and dumb." Other prisoners were forced to wear large signs around their necks that read: "I am a Moron!" As a direct result of the 14f13 program, at least twenty thousand sick and disabled prisoners were transferred from the concentration camps and exterminated in the gas chambers at Bernburg, Hartheim, and Sonnenstein.[55]

The program began in Sachsenhausen, then moved on to Buchenwald, Auschwitz, and Mauthausen, where prisoners were deceived into believing they were being relocated to "rest homes." When the physicians completed their "work" at those camps, they moved on to Dachau, Ravensbruck, Flossenburg, and Neuengamme, where they "weeded out" more than twelve thousand "sick" and "asocial" prisoners.[56] In March 1942 a secret SS directive was sent out to camp commandants instructing them that prisoners who were sick but able to work were not to be killed. One month later, as more camp inmates were needed for armaments work to help fuel the German war effort, commandants were instructed that only "the mentally ill" were to be selected for "mustering out" (*Ausmusterung*) since even "cripples" could be forced to work.[57]

MEDICAL EXPERIMENTATION

The Nuremberg war crimes trials revealed to the world that the Nazis had conducted barbaric experiments on thousands of people with disabilities. Yet few people are aware that the Nazi regime's first medical experiments took place not in concentration camps during the war but in hospitals and research laboratories during Hitler's first years in power. Some of the most gruesome experiments were conducted immediately after the 1933 enactment of the Law for the Prevention of Offspring with Hereditary Diseases, which resulted in the forced sterilization of more than a half-million German nationals. Such experiments were conducted to develop more efficient and inexpensive methods of mass sterilization that could be widely implemented among the disabled and the "inferior" races. The two main methods of sterilization used in these experiments were exposure to radiation and the injection of chemicals into the female reproductive tract.[58]

The first method, developed by Viktor Brack and Horst Schumann, was designed to achieve mass sterilization in what was referred to as the "counter program." Candidates for sterilization were summoned to a government office and, while they stood at a counter filling out registration forms, an x-ray machine hidden behind the counter was turned on and pointed at the subjects' genitals. Exposure for two to three minutes was sufficient to cause permanent sterilization. According to Dr. Leo Alexander, this method failed "because experiments carried out on 100 male prisoners brought out the fact that severe x-ray burns were produced on all subjects. In the course of this research," Alexander continued, "the testicles of the victims were removed for histologic examination two weeks later. I myself examined four castrated survivors of this ghastly experiment. Three had extensive necrosis of the skin near the genitalia, and the other an extensive necrosis of the urethra."[59]

Additional radiation experiments began in the winter of 1942 in Block 10 at Birkenau, the Auschwitz death camp, and at Ravensbruck, a major women's concentration camp north of Berlin.[60] Block 10 at Birkenau was also known as "Clauberg's Block," so named for Dr. Claus Clauberg, who conducted brutal experiments there in hopes of finding a quick and inexpensive means of mass sterilization. Clauberg selected as his subjects married women between the ages of twenty and forty who had borne at least one child. His experiments typically began with the infection of an opaque liquid into a woman's uterus in order to determine by x-ray whether there was any blockage, scarring, or damage to the fallopian tubes. He then injected chemicals into the uterus in order to create infections that would lead to scarring of the tubes within six weeks. The chemicals usually destroyed the membrane of the womb and seriously damaged both ovaries, which were removed and sent to Berlin for examination. Many of Dr. Clauberg's young female subjects died as a result of his experiments. Those who refused to be experimented upon or who resisted were sent to the gas chamber. The women who survived the experiments but became disabled as a result were also sent to death camps and gassed. One female survivor recalled being taken into a dark room by Dr. Clauberg:

> Clauberg ordered me to lie down on the gynecological table and I was able to observe Sylvia Friedman who was preparing an injection syringe with a long needle. Dr. Clauberg used this needle to give me an injection in my womb. I had the feeling that my stomach would burst with the pain. I began to scream so that I could be heard through the entire block. Dr. Clauberg told me roughly to stop screaming immediately, otherwise I'd be taken back at once to the Birkenau concentration camp.[61]

Professor Clauberg later claimed that the methods he developed enabled him to sterilize one thousand women a day.

Equally savage experiments were conducted on people with disabilities at Auschwitz under the direction of Dr. Josef Mengele. Some of these experiments involved the use of dwarfs. Beginning at the age of two, dwarfs selected for such experiments were subjected to anthropological measurements and a variety of brutal clinical tests. After a while, Mengele would kill the dwarfs by injecting chloroform into their hearts, then conduct autopsies and pathological examinations on their internal organs. The supposed purpose of these experiments was to discover the hereditary causes of dwarfism in order to prevent its occurrence among German offspring. One Auschwitz physician later recalled: "Doctor Mengele and his comrades dreamt that the skeletons of the dwarfs and cripples murdered at Auschwitz would one day

stand on special pedestals with cards stating precise information . . . in the spacious corridors of museums."[62]

One Jewish family, the Ovitch family, which consisted of
seven dwarf siblings, traveled throughout Eastern Europe,
performing variety shows to full houses in Czechoslovakia,
Hungary, and Romania. In 1944 the family was rounded up
by the Germans and sent off to Auschwitz to be gassed. Perla
Ovitch was one of the daughters who managed to survive.
The journalist Yehuda Koren recently published an article
about Ms. Ovitch's family:

> In May 1944, more than 430,000 Hungarian Jews were
> marched to the railway stations, to be deported to death
> camps. . . . The Ovitch family was given a horse and car-
> riage to take them to the train. One brother, Leon, who
> was not a dwarf, was not with them; he was trying to hide,
> using false documents. He was executed and his wife and
> baby daughter were later gassed in Auschwitz. When the
> [rest of the] Ovitch family arrived in Auschwitz, they were
> recognized by one of the officers, who stood them aside
> and dashed to alert Dr. Mengele. . . . While the rest of their
> fellow passengers were herded straight to the gas chambers,
> the dwarfs stood by a fence, awaiting their fate. . . . Men-
> gele was delayed and when he eventually arrived the dwarf
> family was no longer there. In the chaotic commotion,
> somebody has already dragged them to the gas chamber.[63]

Ms. Ovitch described what happened next:

> We were standing naked, men and women together,
> when the heavy metal door slammed behind us and we
> started smelling the gas pouring in. I was nauseous and
> we all fell on the floor. Suddenly, through the fog, we

heard shouts coming from outside: "The dwarfs! Where are the dwarfs?"[64]

Suddenly the chamber door opened to reveal Mengele. He ordered the dwarfs to be carried outside and resuscitated. Water was poured over them, and they were given milk to help them vomit the gas. "He [Mengele] was very pleased with us," Ovitch recalled, "and said that we would supply him with work for the next twenty years." Serial numbers were later tattooed on their arms. Perla's number is A 5087.[65]

As Koren explains, Mengele "wanted to discover the secrets of human growth, and here was a living laboratory: seven dwarf siblings and their two normal-size sisters." Although Mengele may have spared their lives, he did not spare them from his savage experiments. Rather, they were kept isolated from the rest of the Auschwitz prisoners in a special barracks where he conducted tests on them and a group of twins. Locked in those barracks for months at a time, Perla and her siblings were subjected to an endless barrage of excruciating procedures:

> Blood was taken from their veins, bone marrow was drawn from their spine, hairs plucked, molars extracted, drops poured into their eyes, blinding them for some hours, hot and cold water pumped into their ears, needles inserted into various nerve centers, electrodes attached to their heads [and] large quantities of various unknown liquids were injected into the wombs of the those dwarf sisters who were married.[66]

What is perhaps most horrifying about Perla Ovitch's story is that she and her siblings, like so many other Europeans with disabilities, were forced to endure brutal experiments while they were alive. Paul Nitsche, a top T4 official, wrote in September 1941 that the Brandenburg-Gorden Asylum was suitable for the study of the feebleminded and epileptics before "disinfection" (the code word for death by gassing). And a staff member at Ravensbruck later recalled that some "abnormal prisoners (mentally ill) were chosen and brought to the operating table, and amputations of the whole leg (at the hip joint) were carried out [as were] amputations of the whole arm." After that, the victims, if they were still alive, "were killed by means of injections," and the legs and arms were "taken to Hohenlyschen . . . for [research] purpose."

Some of Germany's most prestigious research institutions benefited from such horrific experiments by using the harvested body parts of murdered "subjects." Among them were Breslau University, Heidelberg University, and the psychiatric departments at the University of Bonn, Cologne, Berlin, and Leipzig.[67] Paul Nitsche's correspondence with Professor Carl Schneider of the University of Heidelberg resulted from the close association of asylums and university research centers. In October 1942, Schneider wrote of the "many wonderful idiots" he had seen in Professor Dr. August Hirt's Strasbourg laboratory.[68] Three months later, in January 1943, Schneider and Nitsche, began to correspond regarding the brains of dwarfs, twins, and any patients suffering from idiocy or other rare neurological disorders. Schneider selected the brains he wished to study from the registration forms of potential research subjects, which were sent to him by Nitsche. Schneider was apparently very protective of his "research materials," even insisting that the brains be delivered to him personally by courier. Schneider later complained that the asylums were not sending him enough brains and

Prosthetic devices piled up against a wall at Auschwitz. *(Panstwowe Muzeum at Auschwitz-Birkenau)*

suggested that, in order to "increase the material," it was "the turn" of the disabled children to be sacrificed for the "advancement of science."[69]

On March 9, 1944, Schneider's colleague, Professor Hallevorden of the Kaiser Wilhelm Institute for Brain Research in Berlin, acknowledged receipt of 697 brains taken from murdered disabled victims at Brandenburg-Gorden. Historians have also revealed that much of the research of Nazi neurologist Heinrich Gross was based on the preserved brains of children who were killed by Nazi doctors. Some doctors accused of these killings continued to use the remains of their victims for research until the mid-1960s.[70]

Nazi experiments on disabled patients were conducted on the personal initiatives of Nazi physicians, who were given complete freedom to act without regard for human life. As Michael Burleigh notes with tragic irony, "having decimated the [entire German and Polish] asylum population . . . the T-4 psychiatrists, only belatedly realized that this might put them out of a job" and "vainly tried to salvage what they could through macabre experiments on the remains of their victims."[71]

FORCED LABOR

Those persons with disabilities who escaped death or medical experimentation were exploited for their labor. The extent to which a disabled person was able to work often determined whether that individual would live or die. The majority of people with disabilities were able to perform at least some kind of manual labor, and, like many Jewish victims, were brutally exploited for their labor before being killed.[72]

People with disabilities were considered a good labor source because many of them were clustered in institutions and thus could be quickly conscripted in groups for industrial or other work assignments. For example, in 1941 and 1942 the Meseritz-Obrawalde Hospital in the Prussian province of Pomerania received patients with disabilities in transports from at least twenty-six German cities. The staff immediately killed those patients who were unable to work. In addition, slave workers were often imported from the East and then killed once their disability or illness reached the stage where it prevented them from working. As a result of deplorable living and working conditions, many *Ostarbeiter* (imported forced laborers from Poland and the Soviet Union) contracted tuberculosis and were no longer able to work. These people were labeled "mentally ill" and sent to extermination centers where they were gassed to death or given lethal injections.[73]

Both before the T4 program began and after it ended, the use of institutionalized patients as a forced labor source was a widely accepted practice that was usually conducted under the pretense of "therapy." When the euthanasia program began in 1940, staff members demanded productive labor from the remaining patients, and the decision to murder disabled patients was based largely on whether they could work. T4 policy required physicians to report patients with certain conditions if those patients were unable to do work in the institution or could do only routine labor.[74]

As a result of these policies, the institutionalized disabled population was divided into three categories: (1) those who were incurable but still able to work; (2) those able to perform labor as part of "treatment"; and (3) those incurable and no longer able to work. "Work" was very broadly defined. It included "simple mechanical work," which included "the peeling of potatoes and vegetables, the manufacture of simple cardboard boxes, paper bags, and mats, etc." Because the ability to work was the single most important criterion for selecting who was to live or die, "productive" patients temporarily escaped death so that their labor could be exploited and used to fuel the German war machine.[75]

The unpaid labor of disabled patients also allowed German and Austrian institutions to save money on salaried staff and on sedative expenditures since physically exhausted patients tended to be easily manageable. These institutions also profited from the forced labor of their patients. Eglfing-Haar, for example, had 458,691 hectares of land that needed to be cultivated. Institutions also subcontracted work from local industry, such as cigar manufacturers.[76]

After the war, a former inmate of the Eichberg institution who was later transferred to several concentration camps testified that her experiences at Eichberg had been as terrible as her incarceration in the camps. Both disability institutions and concentration camps had slave labor, built-in crematoriums, gas chambers disguised as shower rooms, and starvation wards. Because of these similarities, the terrible strain experienced by patients in institutions were not unlike those experienced by prisoners in concentration camps. For example, Selmar S., an eighteen-year-old patient at the Hadamar killing center, escaped from his work party while laboring on the Schnepfenhausen estate. His threats to "tell things about the asylum" led to his murder in June 1943. Similarly, Minna H., a German woman who was "terrified out of her wits by air raids," was sent forcibly to a German mental institution, where she sewed borders around rugs. In March 1944 she was put to death for being a "trouble-maker" after she requested thimbles for herself and others whose fingers were raw and bleeding from endless hours of sewing.[77]

Deaf people were particularly exploited because their hearing loss did not diminish their ability to perform even the most rigorous physical jobs. In some cases, deaf workers were considered especially desirable because of their ability to function in high-noise industrial or military settings. Some, such as deaf survivor Fred Fedrid, were kept alive specifically to work as skilled labor. Fedrid had been trained as a tailor and was used by the Nazis to alter the uniforms of dead Nazi soldiers for new recruits. His value to the Nazis as a skilled laborer allowed him to survive Auschwitz and Dachau. Rose

Feld-Rosman, a person with a hearing disability, was forced to sew uniforms in a factory. According to the rules of that factory, all workers who broke five needles were sent to be killed in concentration camps. Under unbearable pressure, Feld-Rosman was forced to keep sewing for months after she had broken four needles.[78]

People with disabilities were also conscripted in large numbers from the concentration camps to be part of the slave labor force for German industry. At the Nazi death camp in Auschwitz, for example, I. G. Farben ran a slave-labor plant in which more than 83,000 people worked in 1944. And one company, Siemens, used almost 100,000 men and women in its forced labor program between 1939 and 1945. Siemens obtained most of its work force from among the prisoners of at least 20 death camps set up by the Nazis, including Auschwitz, Flossenburg, and Gross Rosen.

EXPLOITATION AND PLUNDER

In retrospect, it is clear that the Nazi regime, German industry and various Swiss entities profited substantially from the persecution and exploitation of people with disabilities. According to Hugh Gallagher, the economics of euthanasia for the chronically disabled were widely recognized and discussed. "It was wartime, budgets were sky-high, deficits were extraordinary, [and] health resources were limited," Gallagher wrote. "It was argued that expenditures for long-term care of patients, who might never again be economically productive citizens, made little economic sense in cost/benefit terms as compared with similar expenditures on improved

alth programs to keep the able-bodied healthy." In
, ...rce health-care resources had to be rationed.[79]

The belief that people with disabilities were categorically nonproductive and impoverished is false. Many people with disabilities led normal lives with families, homes, property, and businesses. The exploitation of people with disabilities contributed in multiple ways to the Nazi war effort and substantially enriched the Nazi regime. As we have seen, gold watches, gold fillings, spectacle frames, and other personal assets were plundered from victims; their bodies were used for so-called "medical research"; the families of victims were deceived into paying fraudulent expenses; and savings from exterminating rather than caring for the disabled population were tallied. Moreover, people with disabilities were forced to work under inhumane conditions throughout the Nazi era in disability institutions, concentration camps, local industry, and for the German military.

Even the extermination of people with disabilities contributed to the German war effort and substantially enriched the Nazi regime. Relatives of murdered victims were forced to pay fraudulent expenses not only while their loved ones were institutionalized but long after they were killed. Families were charged (at least through the day of the victim's death) for food, lodging, and "health care." In most cases, families in fact paid beyond the day their loved one was killed because of falsified death certificates. The institutions often falsely added several months onto the lives of patients, generating from two hundred to three thousand extra reichsmarks per patient. And since these patients were starved and neglected in their final days, they incurred little to no actual cost for the institutions. The development of entire starvation wards allowed Germany to benefit financially by literally taking food from the mouths of helpless people. The looting methods developed in euthanasia centers were later used in the concentration camps, which also imprisoned thousands of people with disabilities.[80]

Eradicating these "useless eaters" and "social burdens" ultimately saved the government and the German war machine millions of reichsmarks (RMs). Overall the Nazis expected to save 885,439,800 RMs by September 1, 1951. For example, government officials calculated that each murdered patient would have consumed 700 grams of marmalade a month, with each kilo of marmalade costing 120 reichsmarks. From this they concluded that the extermination program saved 5,902,920 kilos of marmalade, which translated into a savings of 7,083,504 reichsmarks over ten years. Savings were similarly tallied from expenditures for cheese, bread, meat, and other essentials.

Even school textbooks asked German students to calculate such costs as a mathematical exercise. One such "problem" presented in a textbook read as follows: If "[t]he construction of a lunatic asylum costs 6 million reichsmarks, [h]ow many houses @ 15,000 reichsmarks each could be built for that amount?"

Another "problem" read:

> To keep a mental patient costs approximately 4 RMs a day, a cripple 5.50 RMs, a criminal 3.50 RMs. In many cases a civil servant only has about 4 RMs, a salaried employee scarcely 3.50 RMs, an unskilled worker not even 2 RMs a head for their families. (a) Illustrate these figures with the aid of pictures. According to conservative estimates, there

are about 300,000 mentally ill, epileptics, etc. in [asylums in Germany.] (b) How much do these people cost to keep in total at a rate of 4 RMs per [person]? (c) How many marriage loans at 1,000 RMs each could be granted [per annum] from this money?[81]

A similar accounting problem was expressed in an internal T4 document found in Hartheim in 1945:

> Assuming an average daily outlay of 3.50 RMs there hereby results:
>
> • a daily saving of RM 245.955
> • an annual saving of RM 88.543.980
> • assuming a life expectancy of ten years RM 885.439.800.
>   . . .
>
> i.e, this sum will have been, or has already been, saved by 1 September 1951 by reason of the disinfection [extermination] of 70.273 persons which has been carried out to date.

In addition to the routine looting of valuables from murdered disabled victims, the staff in the killing centers would often kill patients merely to plunder their assets. One witness recalls "Sometimes the nursing staff just wanted to lay hands upon a watch, a nice suit or a good pair of shoes belonging to a patient, who was then killed to satisfy their cupidity."[82]

The looting methods developed in euthanasia centers were later used in the concentration camps, which also held disabled people. Switzerland reaped direct and substantial benefits from the Nazi persecution and exploitation of people with disabilities. German officials laundered stolen money through Swiss banks by offering looted assets at discount prices in exchange for secure deposits. In order to finance intelligence operations, the German Foreign Office also deposited in Swiss banks funds extorted by the Gestapo and profits from sales of looted diamonds and gold. Essentially the Swiss safeguarded the profits of slave labor and the vast sums of money that the Nazis looted from their victims.[83]

KILLING JEWS WITH DISABILITIES

As Henry Friedlander discusses, Viktor Brack lied under oath at Nuremberg when he testified that no Jews with disabilities had been killed in the euthanasia centers. Like Brack, hundreds of rank-and-file doctors involved in the euthanasia killings deliberately lied when asked about the fate of their Jewish patients. Even today their "lies continue to . . . obscure our understanding of the fate of handicapped Jews" in the Nazi euthanasia program.[84]

Until Hitler assumed power, Jews with disabilities were patients at both Jewish institutions, like the Jacoby Hospital and Nursing Home, and non-Jewish German and Austrian hospitals. Jewish patients with disabilities had also been served by numerous old-age and nursing homes in Jewish communities throughout Germany. As the Third Reich gained power, however, the treatment of Jewish people with disabilities in Germany worsened. By 1939 the Jacoby Hospital, the only Jewish institution serving people with psychiatric disorders, had been "acquired" by the Reich Association of Jews in Germany.[85]

The shifting of responsibility for the care of Jews with disabilities had actually begun in November 1938, with the Reich Ministry of the Interior, Labor, and Finance issuing a decree stating that Jews were entitled only to assistance from Jewish welfare agencies. It did have the caveat that the public welfare agencies would still pay for necessities like shelter, clothing, and medical care, but only if the private Jewish agencies were not able to cover the costs. A new decree in July 1939 reduced the aid to Jews in need even further by stating that not only would Jews be limited to receiving welfare only from private Jewish organizations, which by that time were all funded by the Reich Association of Jews in Germany, but that association would also be responsible for financing the education of all Jewish children. These decrees severely limited the funding available to care for Jews with disabilities in Germany.[86]

In addition to the problem of drastically restricted welfare payments, in the late 1930s Jewish patients with disabilities also began to face discrimination and exclusion from non-Jewish private institutions. Church groups like the Catholic Charity Association or Protestant Home Mission ran many of the non-Jewish institutions. Although Jewish patients had always been welcomes in these institutions, a decision by the German Supreme Administrative Court for Finances in 1937 stating that "nonprofit exemption cannot be granted to institutions and for purposes designed to benefit Jews" changed their policies. The nonprofit Christian hospitals closed their doors to Jews, arguing that threat of losing their nonprofit status compelled them to keep Jews out.[87]

In fact Jews with disabilities were always included in the eugenic "mercy deaths" of this period since extermination was the most powerful and extreme way to exclude people from German society. While the exact number of Jews killed in the T4 program will never be known, scholars like Friedlander have concluded that the number certainly exceeds several thousand, and probably is close to 5,000. This figure is reached by combining the approximately 2,500 publicly institutionalized Jews who were accounted for by the Reich Association of Jews in 1940 and the Jewish patients who were in private institutions, those living in Austria, and those who were not involved with the Reich Association.[88]

Just over a year later, the German government placed further restrictions on the care of the institutionalized Jews. Emphasizing the supposed "danger of race defilement," the Ministry of the Interior demanded that Jews "be physically separated from patients of German or related blood" especially at state hospitals and nursing homes.[89]

The beginning of the "euthanasia" killings also had obvious implications for Jewish patients. As Friedlander argues: "It is inconceivable that handicapped Jews would not have been included in the euthanasia killing operation, but that is exactly what Brack and other T4 functionaries claimed at Nuremberg. They argued that Jews were excluded from the benefit of 'mercy death' granted German handicapped patients. But they could not deny that in 1940 groups of Jewish patients were transported from German institutions and did not return, as demonstrated by prosecution documents submitted at Nuremberg by the United States that included the transport list of Jews taken from Eglfing-Haar."[90]

In the spring of 1940 the Gestapo and then the Ministry of the Interior began collecting detailed information about Jewish patients in institutions. The Ministry of the Interior's letter to institutions specifically asked hospitals and nursing homes to report lists of "Jewish patients suffering from mental illness or feeblemindedness." This series of events marked the decision to begin killing Jewish patients with disabilities in German hospitals. Soon after, in September 1940, Jewish patients were moved out of their institutions and taken to "assembly centers," such as Eglfing-Haar in Bavaria. On September 20 alone, more than 190 Jewish patients with disabilities were collected from institutions. At the time of these transfers, Dr. Herman Pfannmüller sent a list of the names of these transferred Jewish patients to the Ministry of the Interior with a letter stating, "I herewith report to the State Ministry that henceforth my institution will accommodate only Aryan mental patients."[91]

Although there is no documentation of who ordered the Jewish institutionalized patients to be transferred and killed, Friedlander assigns responsibility to Karl Brandt and Philipp Bouhler and adds that they likely discussed the decision directly with Hitler. Jewish people with disabilities were the first Jews to be systematically killed. According to Friedlander, "the decision to kill the handicapped Jewish patients formed an important link between euthanasia and the final solution because it reveals the accelerated efforts to draw more targeted groups into the killing enterprise."[92]

THE BEGINNING OF THE END

Several months before the end of the war, forensic pathologists were sent to an asylum in the city of Obrawalde. Russian troops had reported something amiss at the asylum. By interviewing ten of the patients who who were still alive, and inspecting the facility, the pathologists confirmed that for several years up to fifty patients per day had been killed in the asylum. The pathologists then exhumed the bodies of a sampling of the victims and found morphine and other drugs had been injected into almost all their bodies. By examining the asylum's "death register" the investigators determined that eighteen thousand patients had been murdered at the asylum.[93]

On May 29, 1945, four-year-old Richard Jenne became the last official victim of Nazi euthanasia. He was killed by the staff of the children's ward at Kaufbeuren hospital at 1:10 in the afternoon. His cause of death was listed as "typhus." When American forces investigated Kaufbeuren the next month, they discovered a "wholesale extermination plant" with deplorable conditions. "Scabies, lice, and other vermin were encountered throughout, linens were dirty and quarantine measures non-existent" upon the investigators' arrival.[94]

Although it is impossible to determine precisely how many Europeans with disabilities perished during the Nazi era, the following statistics are usually accepted: adult patients killed as part of the T4 program, 270,000 to 400,000; children in institutions, 5,000 to 10,000; special actions against Jews in institutions, 10,000; concentration camp inmates killed as part of the "Aktion 14f13" program, 20,000 to 40,000.

Deception, denial, and the deliberate destruction of records make precise totals impossible. The same is true concerning the number of people with disabilities murdered at each of the T4 killing centers. For example, Hartheim victims of both ordinary "euthanasia" and killing under the 14f13 program are variously estimated from 20,000 (by Dr. Georg Renno, Lonauer's successor as director), to 400,000 (by Franz Ziereis, the former commandant of Mauthausen, on his deathbed).

But even these figures seem low. Given the fact that Hitler and the Nazi regime were committed to liquidating the entire disabled population in Germany, Austria, Poland, the former Soviet Union, and every occupied territory, it is not unreasonable to suggest that as many as three-quarters of a million people with disabilities were systemically exterminated during the Nazi era.

THREE

Racial Hygiene, Nazi Doctors, and the Sterilization Law

I swear by Apollo Physician, by Asclepius, by
Health, by Panacea, and by all gods and
goddesses, making them my witnesses, that I will
carry out, according to my ability and judgment,
this oath and Indenture. . . . I will use treatment
to help the sick according to my ability and
judgment, but never with a view to injury and
wrongdoing. I will keep pure and holy both my
life and my art. In whatsoever houses I enter, I
will enter to help the sick, and I will abstain from
all intentional wrongdoing and harm. . . . Now if
I carry out this oath, and break it not, may I gain
forever reputation among all men for my life and
for my art; but if I transgress it and forswear
myself, may the opposite be true.

—Oath of Hippocrates

The volkish state must see to it that only the
healthy beget children. . . . Here the state must
act as the guardian of the millennial future. . . .
It must put the most modern medical means in

the service of this knowledge. It must declare
unfit for propagation all who are in any way
visibly sick or who have inherited a disease and
can therefore pass it on.

—Adolf Hitler

The psychiatrist and healthy people are allies
against the genetically defect. The psychiatrist
must render his service in the furtherance of a
hereditary pure, able and superior race.

—Ernst Rudin, German psychiatrist, 1934

SINCE THE 1980S, historians have dramatically increased our
understanding of Nazi racism, which had previously been
conflated with Nazi anti-Semitism. Because of the work of
Robert Proctor, Henry Friedlander, Michael Burleigh, and
others, close attention is now paid to other targets of Nazi
atrocities, including Arab or Afro-Germans ("Rhineland bas-
tards"), homosexuals and lesbians, Sinti and Roma (formerly
called Gypsies), Soviet prisoners of war, and people with disabilities. Our information about Nazi persecution thus now
includes a much greater awareness of the culpability of
various German professionals, including doctors, scientists,
professors, and psychiatrists, in the formation and implementation of Nazi racial policy.[1]

In *Racial Hygiene: Medicine Under the Nazis*, Robert
Proctor shows that the ideological structure associated with
Nazi racism was deeply embedded in the philosophical and
institutional structure of German science long before the

Nazi euthanasia program began in 1939. Proctor carefully documents how German physicians played a leading role in the implementation and execution of Hitler's racialist goals. But in order to understand the crucial role German physicians played in the mass extermination of the disabled, we must first examine the larger social and intellectual context in which they deliberately committed their murderous deeds.[2]

One of the first theoretical expressions of racial ideology was written by the French aristocrat, Joseph Arthur Comte (1816–1882). In his *L'Essai sur l'Inégalité des Races Humaines* (1852), Comte argued that inherent racial inequalities were the "primary motive force of historical development." High cultures were, according to Comte, the work of a master "Aryan" race whose inevitable decline resulted from interbreeding with "inferior" and "lesser" races. In contrast to Comte's largely ignored theories, the publication of Charles Darwin's *Origin of Species* in 1859 marked a major turning point in the development of scientific racism. As Proctor points out, the impact of Darwin's work was enormous, and scholars in Europe and the United States "began to apply the principle of evolution through natural selection to the science of human society." Although Darwinian theory appealed to diverse political constituencies who were "united in the belief that his findings has prescriptive applicability to the science of man," opinions differed over just how Darwin's theory could—and should—be applied.[3]

In the United States, for example, Social Darwinists viewed Darwin's theory as a kind of "scientific guarantee of cosmic optimism": those individuals who survived were, by definition, also the most fit. Implicit in this notion was the assumption that evolutionary theory "demonstrated the moral and political superiority of industrial capitalism and the competitive entrepreneurial spirit." John D. Rockefeller gave voice to this view when he declared that the success of large business in America was "merely the working out of a law of nature and a law of God."[4]

Meanwhile, as Proctor argues, Social Darwinists in Germany were busy justifying their own moral and political order by invoking Darwin's evolutionary theories, but with a dramatically different emphasis. Whereas most late-nineteenth-century American intellectuals expressed great confidence in the "inevitable evolutionary success of the American experiment," their German counterparts tended to emphasize the darker implications of evolutionary theory. Rather than emphasizing the "optimistic laissez-faire, free market liberalism that was embraced in the United States," most German intellectuals stressed the need for aggressive state intervention to prevent what they deemed to be the "inevitable degeneration of the human species." The German eugenics movement that emerged in the late nineteenth century was largely a response to those deep-seated anxieties and fears.[5]

One of the key figures in the early racial hygiene movement in Germany was Ernst Haeckel, who advocated the killing of the "weak" and "mentally defective" in order to strengthen the supposedly superior "Indo-Germanic race."[6] Another key figure in the movement was Alfred Ploetz, who argued that the health of a society, conceived as a genetic collective, should be safeguarded by medical experts who would determine who should be allowed to marry and reproduce. Ploetz also argued against medical care for the "diseased" and "disabled"—who otherwise would not have survived—which allowed those individuals to reproduce and thus contaminate the gene pool.[7] Traditional medical care, Ploetz declared, "helped the individual but ultimately endangered the race." The only solution, according to Ploetz, was a new kind of hygiene—a "racial hygiene" (*Rassenhygiene*)— that would consider "not just the good of the individual but, more important, the good of the race."[8]

Yet it is important to note that the early racial hygiene movement in Germany was not a monolithic or homogenous entity but rather a "diverse blend of both liberals and conservatives, progressives and reactionaries."[9] By the end of World War I, however, "conservative nationalist forces controlled most of the important institutional centers of racial hygiene," and it was this increasingly militant and reactionary right wing of the movement that was ultimately incorporated into the Nazi biomedical apparatus.[10]

A key figure in this transition was Julius Lehmann, a prominent German publisher. During World War I, Lehmann published dozens of military tracts, and in 1918 he assumed publication of *Archiv fur Rassen und Gesellschaftsbiologie*. He also helped found the influential racial hygienist journal *Volk and Rasse* in 1926, and following the Nazi party's rise to power in 1933, published the official commentaries to the Law for the Prevention Offspring with Hereditary Diseases, which called for the compulsory sterilization of persons suffering from certain mental and physical disabilities. As Proctor notes, Lehmann's efforts did not go unrewarded. In 1934 he was the first member of the Nazi party to receive the prestigious Nazi gold medal of honor. Lehmann's rise to prominence also represented an "important shift in the political orientation of the

German racial hygiene movement as forces on the right began to forge an alliance" with racial hygienists.[11]

But perhaps the most important contribution to the German debate on euthanasia was a book published in 1920 by Karl Binding, a professor of law at the University of Leipzig, and Alfred Hoche, a prominent professor of psychiatry at the University of Frieburg. In *Permission for the Destruction of Life Unworthy of Life*, Binding and Hoche argued that the mentally ill should be exterminated for racially hygienic purposes. Binding began his argument by invoking the notion of personal sovereignty. Every individual, Binding declared, possessed inalienable "sovereign powers" to dispose of his or her own life as he or she saw fit.[12]

Binding then delineated three groups of persons that he believed could—and should—be exterminated by the state for the "good" of the state. The first group included terminally ill and severely wounded individuals who expressed the desire to "accelerate the dying process." The second group included all "incurable idiots." The life of "an incurable idiot is absolutely pointless," Binding declared. "They are a terrible, heavy burden upon their relatives and society as a whole and their death would not create even the smallest gap—except perhaps in the feelings of their mothers or loyal nurses." They are, Binding continued, "a travesty of real human beings, occasioning disgust in anyone who encounters them."[13] The third and final group Binding believed should be exterminated were "mentally healthy people, who, having been rendered unconscious by accident, would be appalled to see their own disabled condition if they regained consciousness."[14]

Unlike Binding, Hoche began his argument by citing the dearth of scholarly work on medical ethics. Because there existed no consensus regarding what was medically "ethical," Hoche maintained that instruction in medical ethics must be, by logical necessity, conducted on an informal and ad hoc basis. Everything in medicine was relative, Hoche maintained, including codes of ethics, which "were not to be regarded as something which remains the same for eternity."[15] Hoche then turned his attention to the mentally ill. "Full" and "incurable idiots," he declared, created a "significant burden for the community, their relatives, and the state." They were "mentally dead," mere "human husks," who had "no capacity for suffering" and who were on "an intellectual level which we only encounter way down in the animal kingdom." To show pity or empathy for such "idiots" was therefore illogical, according to Hoche, for "where there was no suffering, there can be no pity" (*wo kein Leiden ist, ist auch keiu mit-Leiden*).[16]

Like many of his contemporaries, Hoche cited economics as a justification for exterminating the disabled. According to Proctor, Hoche claimed that he had "contacted every German asylum in order to establish an average annual cost of 1,300 reichsmarks for the care of each idiot." He then reportedly declared that "twenty to thirty idiots each with a average life expectancy of fifty years represented a massive capital in the form of foodstuffs, clothing, and heating, which is being subtracted from the national product for entirely unproductive purposes." To support his position, Hoche maintained that the state should be thought of as an organic whole, and that any part of the social "body" that was useless or "harmful" should be immediately removed.[17]

Inspired by the ideas of scholars like Binding, Hoche, and Ploetz, Adolf Hitler came to believe that the future volkish state should aggressively pursue pro-natalist policies based upon selective breeding and the eugenic elimination of the unfit in order to maintain the racial purity of the German state. But to achieve these goals, Hitler knew he would need the full support of the German biomedical community. Some scholars have argued that German physicians cooperated with Hitler more than they should have, but that by 1933 it was too late—and too dangerous—for them to dissent or resist. According to this view, the physicians who participated in the Nazi euthanasia program had no choice but to cooperate or flee. But, as Proctor points out, German scientists and physicians "invented" racial hygiene in the first place. Moreover, many of the leading medical journals and institutes advocating racial hygiene were established years before Hitler assumed power in 1933. Indeed, by the early 1930s racial hygiene had already become somewhat of a philosophical and intellectual orthodoxy in Germany, as confirmed by the establishment in 1927 of the Kaiser Wilhelm Institute for Anthropology, Human Genetics, and Eugenics in Berlin.

Part of the research mandate at the Wilhelm Institute provided for "an anthropological survey of the German people and investigations into the heritability of feeble-mindedness, crime, nervous disorders, cancer, tuberculosis, and other human ailments." In 1927, Eugen Fischer was appointed director of the Institute. As director, he not only helped spearhead and supervise research activities that furthered Hitler's racialist goals, he also provided expert advice to top Nazi officials on questions of racial purity. As Proctor shows, Fischer quickly gained prominence in this position and was later named rector of the University of Berlin. At his inaugural address at the University, Fischer publicly praised the Nazis for being "the first to realize that the culture of a people was not the product of its soil or its history alone but was instead the product of the qualities of the race that has given rise to and carried on the culture." Fischer went on to contrast two fundamental philosophies of human health: the "Marxist socialist view which concerns itself with the single individual," and the "National Socialist view which concerned itself with the family." For Fischer it was not individuals who matter but rather sick genetic lines. "Why," he asked, "do we have mandatory registration for contagious diseases such as measles and diphtheria, but not for genetic diseases, such as schizophrenia and mental illness? Why do we know a thousand crippling mutations of the fruit fly *drosophilae* and hardly any in many?"[18]

With men like Fischer leading the German medical community, Hitler was confident he could depend upon the medical profession to help him purify the German race. In a speech before the National Socialist Physicians League, Hitler ingratiated himself with the physicians by declaring that he could, if necessary, do without lawyers, engineers, and builders, but that "you, you National Socialist doctors, I cannot do without you for a single day, not a single hour. If not for you, if you fail me, then all is lost. For what good are our struggles, if the health of our people is in danger?"[19]

On March 21, 1933, less than two months after Hitler was named chancellor of Germany, Dr. Alfons Stauder, head of two major German medical associations, met with several key figures in the National Socialist Physicians League to plan the reorganization of the medical profession to better

TABLE 2

GERMAN DOCTORS AND SCIENTISTS INVOLVED IN
NAZI CRIMES: THE INTELLECTUAL MENTORS[20]

Erwin Bauer (1874–1952)	Chair in Botany, Berlin Agricultural College, and Kaiser Wilhelm Institute (KWI) breeding research
Eugen Fischer (1874–1952)	Chair in Anthropology, Berlin, and KWI anthropology
Hans Gunther (1891–1968)	Chair in Anthropology, Jena, Berlin, Frieburg
Alfred Hoche (1865–1943)	Chair in Psychiatry, Frieburg
Fritz Lenz (1897–1976)	Chair in Racial Hygiene, Munich
Ernst Rudin (1874–1952)	Director, KWI Psychiatry, Munich

conform with Hitler's goals. Shortly thereafter, Stauder sent a telegram to Hitler, pledging the medical profession's unqualified support to the new regime:

> To Reichskanzler Hitler: The medical associations of Germany—the German medical association and the Hartmaannbund—welcome with greatest joy the determination of the Reich government of national reconstruction to create a true volk community of all estates, professions, and classes and place themselves happily in the service of this great task of our fatherland, with the promise faithfully to fulfill our duty as servants of the people's health.[22]

Two weeks later, on April 5, 1933, Hitler asked the German medical profession to move with all its energy to the forefront of the racial hygiene question. The German medical profession did not fail him.

TABLE 3

GERMAN DOCTORS AND SCIENTISTS INVOLVED IN NAZI
CRIMES: THE MEDICAL EXPERTS[21]

Werner Catel	Chair in Pediatrics, Leipzig	Expert for child euthanasia
Max de Crinis	Chair in Psychiatry, Cologne, Berlin	Expert for adult euthanasia
Julius Hallervorden	Director, KWI Brain Research	Brain research on victims
Hans Heinze	Chief, Brandenborg-Gorden	Director, T-4 research center
Werner Heyde	Chair in Psychiatry, Wurzburg	T4 medical director
Berthold Kihn	Chair in Psychiatry, Jena	Expert for adult euthanasia
Friedrich Mauz	Chair in Psychiatry, Konisburg	Expert for adult euthanasia
Paul Nitsche	Chief, Sonnenstein Hospital	T4 medical director
Friedrich Panse	Professor of Psychiatry, Bonn	Medical expert for euthanasia
Kurt Pohlisch	Chair in Psychiatry, Bonn	Medical expert for euthanasia
Carl Schneider	Chair in Psychiatry, Breslau	Medical expert for euthanasia
Werner Villinger	Chair in Psychiatry, Breslau	Medical expert for euthanasia
Konrad Zucker	Professor of Psychiatry, Heidelberg	Brain research on euthanasia victims

THE LAW FOR THE PREVENTION
OF OFFSPRING WITH HEREDITARY DISEASES

In June 1933, Reich Interior Minister Wilhelm Frick announced the formation of an "expert committee" on questions of population policy to help achieve Nazi racialist goals.

At the committee's first meeting, Frick called for a new population policy to combat the "threats" that were endangering the health of the German people. Among Frick's gravest concerns was the "fact" that the number of "genetically diseased" people was rapidly growing in the population due to the lack of aggressive state-administered racial policies.[23]

One month later, on July 14, 1933, the same day Hitler outlawed the formation of political parties, the German government enacted the Law for the Prevention of Offspring with Hereditary Diseases. Passed in the same cabinet session that concluded the concordat with the Vatican, this law sanctioned the compulsory sterilization of persons suffering from a wide variety of supposedly hereditary illnesses, including congenital feeblemindedness, schizophrenia, manic-depressive insanity, genetic blindness or deafness, and severe physical deformities. German physicians were required to report, in exchange for a small fee, all cases that fell within the purview of the law. But, as we shall see, many German physicians needed little encouragement to comply with the law as they had been advocating the need to sterilize the "disabled" for years.

In the early 1890s the German psychiatrist August Forel tried to justify sterilization of the insane as "a national sacrifice similar to that of a soldier in the time of war." Other German medical professionals went further, like the Heidelberg gynecologist Edwin Kehere, who, according to Proctor, sterilized at least one of his patients to ensure that she would no longer bring "inferior" children into the world. In 1903 the German psychiatrist Ernst Rudin proposed the forced sterilization of "incurable alcoholics." And in 1914 bills were introduced into German parliament to legalize voluntary sterilization. By 1930 many German medical and scientific journals were publicly calling for the forced sterilization of the "disabled" and "unfit" for the benefit of the German race.[24] But Germany was not alone in this movement. In September 1928 the Swiss canton of Waadt passed a law under which the "mentally ill" and "feebleminded" could be forcibly sterilized if public health authorities determined that such individuals were "incurable" and likely to produce degenerate offspring. In 1929, Denmark became the second European nation to legalize compulsory sterilization. Five years later Norway passed its own sterilization law, followed by similar laws in Sweden, Finland, Estonia, Iceland, Cuba, Czechoslovakia, Yugoslavia, Latvia, Hungary, and Turkey.[25]

It was in the United States, however, that compulsory sterilization of persons with disabilities was first legalized. In 1907, Indiana passed the first American law allowing sterilization of the mentally ill and criminally insane. By the late 1920s, twenty-eight American states had followed suit, enacting legislation that resulted in the forced sterilization of more than fifteen thousand U.S. citizens before 1930. By 1939 more than thirty thousand Americans in twenty-nine states had been sterilized on eugenics grounds. Nearly half the procedures were carried out in California.[26]

After World War I, German racial hygienists, worried that their "American adversaries might surpass the fatherland in racial health," began proposing increasingly aggressive measures to improve the health and purity of the German race. As Proctor tells us, Dr. Gustav Boeters, a prominent German advocate of involuntary sterilization, publicly defended the forced sterilization of "mental defectives" in 1924 by appealing to nationalistic sentiments: "What we racial hygienists promote is by no means new or unheard of. In a culture nation of the first order—the United States of America—that which we strive toward was introduced and tested long ago. It is all so simple and clear." One year later Otto Reich, chairman of the Vienna Society for Racial Care, expressed his fear that America was quickly becoming the world's leader in racial hygiene and urged Germans to "catch up." Racial care, Reich declared, "must become the foundation of all domestic policy, and at least a part of foreign policy."[27]

Despite the German eugenicists' best efforts, proposals to allow some form of voluntary sterilization were repeatedly rejected by the legislatures of the Weimar Republic. But "progress" in that direction was finally made on July 2, 1932, when a group of prominent members of the German Medical Association met with the Prussian Health Council to discuss "the question of eugenics in the service of the economy." Two months later, in September 1932, the Council voted to approve "limited medically supervised and voluntary sterilization designed to stop the breeding of 'genetic defectives.'" Then, in the fall of 1932, legislation was placed before the German parliament that allowed for voluntary sterilization.[28]

It was a short step from the sterilization law the Weimar government passed in 1932 to the Nazi regime's 1933 Law for the Prevention of Offspring with Hereditary Diseases. The German legislature made it clear, however, that this law was not intended to be punitive. That is, persons ordered to be sterilized were not to be viewed as "perpetrators of a crime for which they were receiving punishment." Rather, forced sterilization, according to its proponents, should be seen as the sacrifice an individual makes as a result of the "personal tragedy" of having been born "defective."[29]

TABLE 4

STERILIZATION APPLICATIONS AND

DECISIONS IN GERMANY, 1934–1936[30]

Year	Applications	Positive decisions	Negative decisions
1934	84,604	62,463	4,874
1935	88,193	71,760	8,976
1936	86,254	64,646	11,619

TABLE 5

STERILIZATION SURGERIES IN GERMANY[31]

Year	Positive decisions	Surgeries performed
1934	62,463	32,268
1935	71,760	73,174
1936	64,646	63,547

TABLE 6

DEATHS RESULTING FROM

STERILIZATION SURGERIES IN GERMANY[32]

Year	Men ster.	Women ster.	Total deaths	Men	Women
1934	16,238	16,030	102	21	81
1935	37,834	35,340	208	35	173
1936	32,887	30,624	127	14	113[33]

Pursuant to the terms of the new law, all German physicians, nurses, and public health officials were required to register every case of genetic illness known to them. Article 9
allowed fines of up to 150 reichsmarks for any doctor who
failed to register such a person. Individuals with disabilities
were usually first recommended for sterilization by their
physicians, who would present an analysis to the local genetic
health courts, the first of which convened in Berlin on March
15, 1934. According to Friedlander, genetic health courts

received 84,525 applications for sterilization between March and December 1934. During that period the courts handed down 64,499 decisions: 56,244 in favor of sterilization and 3,692 against (4,563 were either retracted or postponed). The pace quickened between 1934 and 1939, when the courts decided in favor of sterilization in nearly 95 percent of the cases heard. Individuals who were ordered to be sterilized were guaranteed the right to appeal their decisions to appellate genetic courts, and many did so. In 1934 nearly 4,000 persons appealed their decisions; only 77 were successful. The vast majority (3,559) failed in their attempts to overturn the lower courts' decisions. Throughout the entire Nazi era, fewer than 3 percent of appealed decisions were reversed. Those who refused to submit to sterilization were typically sent to concentration camps where they were killed.[34]

STERILIZING PEOPLE WITH HEARING DISABILITIES

Among the many ailments that fell within the broad scope of the law, "feeblemindedness" was the most common ground for sterilization, followed by schizophrenia and epilepsy. People who were deaf were also primary targets for sterilization; yet, for whatever reason, their stories have rarely been discussed. Although there are no comprehensive studies that examine the application of the sterilization law to the deaf, occasional references do exist. One German historian, for example, has suggested that more than fifteen thousand congenitally deaf persons may have been sterilized under the law. In the early 1990s, Horst Biesold recently tried to substantiate that claim by collecting oral histories from deaf survivors

TABLE 7

STERILIZATIONS CLASSIFIED BY DISEASE, 1934[35]

Diagnosis	Sterilizations (%)	Men sterilized (%)	Women sterilized (%)
Feeblemindedness	17,070 (52.9%)	7,901 (48.7%)	9,169 (57.3%)
Schizophrenia	8,194 (25.4%)	4,261 (26.2%)	3,933 (24.5%)
Hereditary epilepsy	4,520 (14.0%)	2,539 (15.6%)	1,981 (12.4%)
Manic-depressive	1,017 (3.2%)	384 (2.4%)	633 (3.9%)
Alcoholism	775 (2.4%)	755 (4.6%)	20 (0.1%)
Hereditary deafness	337 (1.0%)	190 (1.2%)	147 (0.9%)
Hereditary blindness	201 (0.6%)	126 (0.8%)	75 (0.5%)
Sev. malformations	94 (0.3%)	45 (0.3%)	49 (0.3%)
St. Vitus' Dance	60 (0.2%)	37 (0.2%)	23 (0.1%)

of Nazi sterilization. Biesold later presented his findings in *Crying Hands: Eugenics and Deaf People in Nazi Germany.*[36]

Initial conversations with deaf survivors of Nazi atrocities led Biesold to realize that gaining the confidence and collaboration of deaf persons who had been forcibly sterilized would be difficult for several reasons, including the fact that "race hygienists claims that the hereditary diseased were inferior created a self-perception of worthlessness among congenitally deaf persons." Nevertheless, Biesold sought the cooperation of deaf victims of sterilization by making a public appeal in many of the leading journals and newspapers that deaf people in Europe routinely read. Biesold ultimately received 1,215 responses from deaf people who said they had been sterilized by the Nazi regime. Based upon these responses, Biesold's findings included the following:

1. Fifty-four percent of the surviving victims of forced sterilization were female.

2. Nearly all victims (95 percent) were born between 1901 and 1926.

3. The youngest victim was sterilized when she was 9 years old; the oldest was 50 years old.

4. The most common age was between 22 and 30.

5. The victims named 104 institutions for deaf students as their home school.

6. Compulsory sterilization took place throughout Germany but particularly in cities that contained schools for the deaf.[37]

The testimony Biesold collected indicates that many of the directors at German schools for the deaf actively promoted the sterilization law. Among those institutions that collaborated with the Nazi regime were the Training Institute for Teachers of the Deaf in Berlin-Neukoelln, the Institute for the Deaf in Heidelberg, the Homberg Institute, the Schleswig Institution for the Deaf, the District Instructional and Vocational Institution for Deaf Girls in Dilligen, and the Pauline Home in Winnenden.

BETRAYAL OF THE STUDENTS

The Training Institute for Teachers of the Deaf in Berlin-Neukoelln. Founded in 1788, the Training Institute was not only the oldest but also had become the premier training institute for Prussian teachers of the deaf. Gotthold Lehmann served as principal of the school and director of the teacher training program. In addition to his administrative and teaching duties, Lehmann was responsible for proposing future university courses to the Prussian state ministry in science, art, and public education. During the early Nazi era,

Lehmann proposed several eugenics-related topics for participants in the first-year teachers' program, among them "The Science of Human Heredity and German Race Cultivation," "The Theory of Hereditary and Race Hygiene," and "The Collaboration of the Schools for the Deaf in the Implementation of the Law for the Prevention of Offspring with Hereditary Diseases."[38]

The close affiliation of the school's teacher-training curriculum with Nazi ideology was not coincidental. Lehmann was a member of the National Socialist Teachers Confederation well before the Nazi integration of the Union of German Teachers of the Deaf, and he actively encouraged the implementation of the Sterilization Law at his institution. Not only did he personally inform authorities about certain deaf students under his supervision, he also worked to persuade parents to consent to their children's sterilization. A letter Lehmann wrote on April 14, 1936, to the distressed mother of one of his students illustrates his stance:

> To Frau [NN],
>
> The health authority of Berlin-Neukoelln has informed me by a letter of April 6 1936 that a judgment concerning the sterilization of your daughter has been delivered in accordance with the law and that [NN] is to be conducted within two weeks to the Neukoelln Municipal Hospital for the performance of the operation. I would ask you to sign the enclosed declaration and return it to me. I would point out that thus far fourteen sterilizations have been completed on our children and that in no case have negative effects occurred.
>
> Heil Hitler!

Fewer than four months later, Lehmann wrote again to the mother, who had refused to consent to the sterilization of her daughter. "Dear Frau NN," Lehmann wrote, your daughter "was released from the clinic in good health on August 16. The operation proceeded normally. . . . The law stipulates that in the case of persons above fourteen years of age, the operation may be performed without the consent of parents and guardians. You could not then have changed anything in this regard. I believe that it will be quite a good thing for [NN] that she has no children. Her life will likely be hard enough as it is."[39]

A former student of Lehmann's described how violence was sometimes used when pupils resisted sterilization. Soon after his fourteenth birthday in November 1938, a male student was told that he would be sterilized at the Rudolf Virchow hospital in Berlin after the recommendation of one of his teachers. On the boy's third unsuccessful attempt to escape from the school, he was seized by the police, handcuffed, beaten, and then taken to the hospital where he was castrated.[40]

The Institute for the Deaf in Heidelberg. Equally brutal practices occurred at the Institute for the Deaf in Heidelberg. The director of that school, Edwin Singer, worked closely with the university's ear, nose, and throat clinic, and with the resident physician at the institution, Dr. W. Hoffman. One former student, who was fifteen at the time of his sterilization, described his experiences at Heidelberg: "While the other students from the residential school for the deaf in Heidelberg went on holidays, I and a few other deaf students were taken away on the orders of the principal for compulsory sterilization. I wanted to run away, but I knew that I didn't have a chance. They threatened to have me brought back by the police. Just before the operation, I cried a great deal because I felt so powerless."[41] After the war, Singer never expressed remorse over what he had done to his former students. In a 1946 article he crudely explained that it was "not seemly to dwell on the ruins." Even in his old age, Singer would neither apologize nor admit to the inhumanity of his deeds. In 1960 a former student wrote to Singer, asking him why he had sent him to be sterilized.[42]

"Dear Director Edwin Singer," the man wrote. "When I came to the city hospital on Wednesday April 10 1935, I did not know what I was doing there. Then I lay in bed for only two days, until Friday, when the national socialist doctor, Herr Karl Gamstader, said that I would be operated on at 10 am that same day. This assistant doctor sterilized my abdomen in the cruelest fashion and made me infertile. On April 20 1935 I was released from the city hospital. On the way home," he continued,

> I was faint with weakness. I felt so tormented and cruelly treated because I hadn't been told anything. Why did you keep silent and not tell me that sterilization would mean killing my body and that it is wrong and a crime that I cannot have children? You also abused my brother NN and Frau NN and NN. You didn't warn us. We are not content with you professionally because of your offenses and disregard. Sterilization makes a body worthless. I no longer feel like a real person. . . . Why did I have to be sterilized? . . . You would rather kill my belly and have me sterilized and keep silent, than let me know openly that I could not have

a child. . . . A great deal has been lost from my life, because there can be never be any happy love. . . . For you, the word human is no longer applicable . . . you are guilty of a crime toward me. You abused me. You had me sterilized, killed and destroyed me so that I can't have a child. You did not really understand what a human being is.[43]

Singer, even at eighty-one years old, was not moved. "The fact that you have no children," he wrote bluntly, "should not be seen as a misfortune. Better to have no children, than one who is blind or deaf or epileptic."[44]

Homberg Institution. In 1933 a staff of sixteen teachers taught a small group of deaf students at Homberg Institution. Nazi party member Oskar Ronigk was the principal of the school. Former students later recalled that Ronigk was a very strict man who routinely reported his students to the Nazi health authorities for sterilization. Ronigk's decisions about which children to report to the authorities were guided by the responses on the school's registration form, which required parents or guardians to list the child's "physical condition" and "causes for deafness." A notation of hereditary deafness always led to sterilization. Ronigk followed the lead of his fellow Nazi party members who used genealogical charts of his students' families to "conduct research on hereditary diseases and the conditions of genetic transmission in families." On September 20, 1934, he sent letters to the parents of all students enrolled at the school, instructing them "to complete the enclosed genealogical charts conscientiously and to return to the institution by Easter 1935 at the latest." Ronigk then used the information to determine which students would be sterilized.[45]

The Schleswig Institution for the Deaf. The Schleswig Provincial Institution for the Deaf was founded by Georg Pfingsten in 1787 and by 1931 the school had 14 staff members and 121 deaf students. After Hitler's rise to power, a Nazi party member and teacher of the deaf named Mr. Heidebrede was named director of the school. Based in part on his experiences at a Nazi training camp, he urged parents and teachers in his quest to implement Nazi policies at the school. He sent the following letter to parents of students enrolled at his school:

> The agencies responsible for the implementation of the Law for the Prevention of Offspring with Hereditary Disease of July 14, 1933, may expect accurate information from us concerning the deaf children who fall under the provisions of the law. In accordance with section 1, paragraph 2, of the law, these are persons suffering from *hereditary* deafness. Our personal and medical questionnaires give us only scanty information on the *cause* of deafness, since they aim only to determine the educability of the child, and in this regard the distinction between inherited and adventitious deafness is of little consequence. We would [therefore ask] you to help us complete the missing information on the enclosed questionnaires with answers as detailed as possible. The information is unconditionally required for the complete and successful implementation of the law. We know that we have set you no light or welcome task, but we hope that you will gladly take this opportunity to collaborate in the improvement of the German people, which is the ultimate objective of this law. Your cooperation will be of value in completing the work of our führer Adolf Hitler; in his

vision, as we know, race hygiene thought is a cornerstone in the formation and expansion of the Third Reich. . . . Heil Hitler![46]

Based upon the information provided on the questionnaires, Heidebrede reported dozens of his young students to Nazi health authorities, who summarily sterilized the children without parental notification or consent.[47]

The District Instructional and Vocational Institution for Deaf Girls in Dilligen. In 1931 ninety-eight Catholic girls were enrolled in the District Instructional and Vocational Institution for Deaf Girls in Dilligen. In 1936 a thirteen-year-old deaf girl, who was living at the institution and working as a baker's assistant, received a letter instructing her voluntarily to submit to a sterilization operation. The girl objected to the procedure, citing section 6 of the ordinance for the implementation of the law, which provided:

> If the subject has been admitted at personal expense to a private institution that offers a full guarantee that reproduction will not occur, the law stipulates that on the subject's application the completion of the operation may be deferred as long as the subject is living in this or a similar institution. If the subject is legally incapacitated or has not yet reached eighteen years of age, the legal guardian is authorized to make such an application. If a deferral occurs before the eighteenth birthday, the subject may after that date make a personal application for further exemption.[48]

The girl was thus fully within her rights under the law to refuse to submit to the operation because she was living and working at a private institution. But since she had not yet reached her eighteenth birthday, she was required to ask her guardian, Dr. Hogen, who was also the mayor of the city of Dilligen, to apply for an exemption from the operation. Terrified, the girl turned to Hogen for help. But he ignored the exemption provision related to private institutions in his decision, explaining that because he was the girl's guardian, section 6 of the ordinance justified his use of coercive measures. Hogen later made the following notation on the back of his decision: "Matter settled. [NN] was committed to the Gunzberg Hospital on December 14, 1936."[49]

The Pauline Home in Winnenden. At the Pauline Home in Winnenden, there was a vocational school for the deaf where students received training as basket makers, tailors, shoemakers, and brush makers. Of the seventy-six student records available for examination, forty-one children were reported to Nazi officials under the terms of the sterilization law. But these figures do not reveal the fervor with which the superintendent of the school, Pastor Muller, a member of the Nazi party and a faithful adherent to Nazi ideology, worked to send the young children under his "care" to their Nazi tormentors.[50]

Muller's desire to ensure that his pupils were sterilized can be seen in the proceedings surrounding a young girl who was to be discharged after successfully completing her vocational training. The provincial youth health officer in Stuttgart, Dr. Eyerich, examined her case and he initially concluded that the girl's mother was "physically and mentally inferior." Muller also indicated in the girl's file that her father was "of modest mental endowment." The attending physician, however, disagreed: "The father . . . does not make an unfavorable impression on me, but he is very hard of hearing."[51]

Apparently the parents had stated that their daughter was born with full hearing but had been deafened at the age of seven after an accident, in which she was run over by a beer wagon. Muller did not believe this testimony and tried to persuade the physician to sterilize the girl by defaming her character. "According to the report of the director of the Institution," Eyerich wrote, "she is not a good worker and is very frivolous, is out after men, has an acquaintanceship with a deaf man in Feuerbach, but also flirts with the deaf in the Institution." After several days Dr. Eyerich handed down the decision Muller was hoping for:

> Diagnosis: congenital deafness. The question of whether deafness is of heredity nature cannot be unequivocally answered. In all probability, it is a question of deafness as the consequence of congenital lues [syphilis]. Consequently the girl is not to be characterized as hereditably diseased in the sense of the law. Nonetheless, I recommend sterilization since our findings suggest that lues is probably not the single cause of her inferiority and, in addition, the father is extremely hard of hearing. Both the father and mother are mentally inferior. It must be concluded that the risk in NN having children is very great and that, in the event of reproduction, one must certainly reckon with inferior offspring. In addition, she would be completely incapable of raising a child in proper fashion.[52]

Dr. Eyerich's "expert opinion" was submitted along with his recommendation to the Stuttgart I district court on December 7, 1934. Shortly thereafter, the young girl was sterilized.[53]

In another case, the parents of a fourteen-year-old girl living at the Pauline Home were notified of their daughter's sterilization three days after the operation had been performed with only the following letter.

> Dear Herr [NN], We should like to inform you that by order of the hereditary health court your daughter has been in Waiblingen district hospital since Wednesday for a sterilization operation. It is indicated that she will return to us by the middle or end of next week. With best regards and Heil Hitler!"[54]

While the Nazi doctors and administrators who participated in the sterilization program later tried to minimize the severity of the procedures, the impact on the victims was devastating, as evidenced by the following accounts that Horst Biesold collected from Nazi survivors:

Female, born 1918

I was forcibly sterilized by the Nazis in July 1938. It was an extremely painful torture, the doctor bored around in the sensitive part of my vagina with his finger. I suffered terrible pain. . . . Throughout my marriage with a deaf husband I have had pains as a result of the operation. Even today the pains are often very intense. Almost always I have pain during intercourse with my husband. While other women have orgasms and experience the joy of lovemaking, the pain from the operation scars kills all pleasure for me. It caused me a lot of grief that I could not have a child. All the people whom I get to know well ask me why I don't have any children.[55]

Female, born 1914

I too belong to the forcibly sterilized. My ancestors had absolutely not transmitted any hereditary diseases. My fiancé at the time also told me that I was not genetically defective. A year later, in 1935, I was very badly disillusioned by the health authority in Osnabruck. About three months after the operation, my fiancé said to me that we had to break up; he couldn't be expected to keep a wife with a "Hitler cut" for the rest of his life.[56]

Male, born 1917

In 1935 I was an apprentice cabinetmaker. After my adamant refusal, I was hauled away by force by the Gestapo from the workshop in xx and immediately delivered to the hospital in xx. There I was forcibly sterilized. My deaf brother bb was not sterilized, thanks to the second world war. He had two healthy children. My sister, happily married, also had seven healthy children. I still suffer from it, and question why it was just me who had to suffer a fate with such terrible consequences.[57]

Female, born 1920

When I was fifteen I was brought to xx to be sterilized. Unfortunately, I have no witnesses, just the scar on my abdomen. . . . With time, the abdominal pains were replaced by pains of the heart when my fiancé backed out of the marriage because I could no longer have children. That happened to me three times, so that I withdrew more and more from life. . . .[58]

Female, born 1920

I am writing you now that I am so lonesome without children. My husband died in 1981. I am very unhappy. Why were the Nazis so cruel as to sterilize me? I wanted to have at most two children. I was scarcely seventeen years old when I was forced to go the hospital in . . . east Prussia to be sterilized.[59]

The Nazi sterilization program was largely brought to an end with the outbreak of war. Only about 5 percent of all sterilizations were performed after 1939, the year that marked the beginning of the T4 euthanasia program in which thousands of deaf people were brutally killed. A deaf dressmaker, identified only as "C.W." and as a mother of a hearing-disabled daughter, provides just one example of the fate of deaf people under the Nazi regime's euthanasia program. German health authorities detained C.W. at the age of thirty and ordered her sterilization on July 17, 1937. Four years later C.W. was transferred from her workplace to a psychiatric hospital in Munster, where in the summer of 1941 she was murdered. Her death certificate listed her cause of death as a "weak heart."[60]

A forcibly sterilized deaf woman who was taken from her school and sent to Hadamar when she was a teenager provides another example of Nazi atrocities committed against the deaf. On July 26, 1941, the deaf woman's sister received a letter from the director of the Elmendorf Remedial Training Institute:

> By order of the Reich Defense Commissioner, your sister, NN, . . . was transferred on July 25, 1941 by the Charitable Patient Transport Company . . . to another institution whose name and address are not known to me. The receiving institution will send you a corresponding communication. I would ask you to abstain from further inquires until this notice is received. . . .[61]

Two weeks later, on August 1, 1941, the woman's sister received another letter from the director of the so-called Provincial Hospital and Nursing Home in Hadamar. "Dear NN," the letter read. "We inform you that your sister, NN, by ministerial order on the directions of the Reich Defense Commissar, has been transferred to our institution and has arrived safely. At this time visits cannot be permitted for reasons associated with Reich defense and similar telephone communications cannot be answered. Any other changes that occur in the condition of the patient or in connection with the ban on visits will be communicated to you at once. The additional work that has been caused by these measures forces us to ask kindly that you abstain from further inquires. . . . Heil Hitler!"[62] Three weeks later the sister received one final letter:

Dear Frau NN,

Subsequent to our letter of August 1, 1941 we inform you with regret that your sister, Frau NN, who had to be transferred to our institution in connection with measures ordered by the Reich Defense Commissar, unexpectedly died on August 18, 1941 as a consequence of pulmonary tuberculosis with an associated attack of military tuberculosis. Since our institution is designated only as a transit center for those patients who are to be transferred to another institution in the region and they stay here only to identify carriers of infection, who, as is well known, are always to be found among such patients, the responsible local police authority has ordered the immediate cremation of the remains and the disinfection of belongings in order to prevent the outbreak and transfer of infectious diseases. In these cases the agreement of relatives is not required. Belongings brought to the institution, will, after disinfections, be retained as security for the bearer of costs. We would inform you kindly to note that damage to personal belongings from the powerful agents employed in disinfecting can very often not be avoided. Usually both shipment and the drafting of a decision concerning the allocation of the patient's belongings cost more time and money than the belongings are worth. May we ask you to consider whether it is possible for you to renounce claims to these belongings, so that . . . we can refer them to National Socialist Public Welfare and to otherwise needy inmates of the institution. In the event that you wish the urn to be buried in a specific cemetery—transport of the urn is without cost . . . [however] surrender of the urns to private individuals is not permissible by law. If you do not send us this notification within fourteen days, an alternate burial will be carried out, and we shall also assume that you abstain from any claim on the belongings. . . . We enclose a death certificate for submission to the authorities. Heil Hitler![63]

Those who managed to survive the sterilization process were burdened with feelings of irreversible violation of their physical integrity. The traumatic experience of compulsory sterilization also caused the end of many marriages. In addition, nearly one-quarter of those surveyed said their forced sterilization caused them to remain unmarried. Consequently these survivors suffered chronic "anxiety at having to grow old without the supportive love of children, and an uncertain future in isolation and loneliness." Many survivors also lived under a cloak of secrecy and a deep sense of shame and inferiority instilled in them by their Nazi tormentors.[64]

Finally, by being forcibly sterilized, people with disabilities were not only deprived of the treasured ability to have children, they also lost the chance to add loved ones to a burgeoning disability culture. For example, in the early 1930s Germany had a remarkably advanced deaf culture that flourished in deaf educational institutions and retirement homes. By forcibly sterilizing thousands in the deaf community and by working to death many more, the Nazis nearly destroyed the deaf community (and prevented the deaf from perpetuating a rich cultural heritage through their children). The deaf community of Germany has yet to recover fully from its almost complete annihilation by the Nazi regime.

Nearly seventy years after the German government began sterilizing its first victims, eugenic and discriminatory attitudes continue to degrade and victimize people with disabilities in countries throughout the world. As Professor Jacques Voneche, a specialist in child and adolescent psychology at the University of Geneva, explains: "Obviously, these sterilizations are still being practiced today in Switzerland, but not openly." Voneche suggests that forced sterilizations are supported by parents, doctors, and leaders of various institutions. Authorities have denied these allegations, and the Swiss government has evaded responsibility by arguing that the twenty-six cantons of the Swiss federation are each responsible for making their own decisions on public health.

FOUR

Perpetrators and Accomplices

I was ordered to do it. When I am asked again,
why I didn't refuse, although I realized that it
was an injustice, I can't give an answer to this
question. I do and did in the past have a strong
feeling of guilt, but it is impossible for me to give
a reason for the fact that I didn't refuse. It simply
was ordered and I had to execute the orders.

—Erna Elfriede, a nurse accused
of killing two hundred patients

I never thought about that question. After
[Arthur] Nebe told me that he had orders to kill
the mental patients in his area, there was nothing
for me to think about.
—Albert Widmann, T4 chemist

T4 MANAGERS

ALTHOUGH Nazi doctors played the central role in the
killing of patients with disabilities, there were thousands of
managers, supervisors, nurses, chemists, and researchers who
also played crucial roles in the euthanasia programs. Not

including the physicians, the T4 program was managed by sixteen men: Viktor Brack, Werner Blankenburg, Dietrich Allers, Hans-Joachim Becker, Gerhard Bohne, Friedrich Haus, Hans Hefelmann, Richard von Hegener, Adolf Kaufmann, Friedrich Lorent, Arbold Oels, Fritz Schmiedel, Willy Schneider, Gerhard Siebert, Friedrich Tillmann, and Reinhold Vorberg. As Henry Friedlander explains, all of these men, save possibly Schmiedel, were in their twenties or thirties when Hitler assumed power in 1933. All were raised in modest, middle-class families. Moreover, most of the T4 managers were well educated and five had earned advanced degrees. The others attended secondary school and thereafter received business training of some sort, except Kaufmann, who was trained as a mechanic. But, perhaps most important, none of the men were well established in their careers when the Nazis assumed power.[1]

For these managers, their jobs in the T4 program provided access to power and the possibility of career advancement within the Nazi regime. Their recruitment and selection depended on a variety of factors, including party credentials, friendship, skills, and family connections. Brack, for example, advanced from being Himmler's personal driver to serving as Bouhler's assistant, and when Bouhler helped to establish the Führer's chancellory (KdF), he appointed Brack as his deputy. Vorberg was Brack's cousin, and von Hegener was the brother-in-law of Hans Reiter, president of the Reich Health Office. The other men were recruited to the program based largely on party loyalty and personal connections.[2]

The T4 managers have often been described by scholars as "bureaucratic killers"—or, in German, *Schreibtischtäter,* which translates as "desk murderers" in English.

Some scholars argue that the job of these bureaucrats consisted of minor steps in the overall killing process. But, as Friedlander argues, this analysis "implies a greater distance from the killing fields than was actually true." Brack, Blankenburg, Bohne, Hefelmann, von Hegener, and Vorberg, for example, all were present at the first experimental gassing at Brandenburg. And Kaufmann not only helped install gas chambers and crematoria, he also hired the non-medical staff at five of the six killing centers and routinely inspected those centers to assure the secrecy and efficiency of the killing process. Similarly, Dietrich Allers visited the T4 centers numerous times, and Vorberg resided for months at Grafeneck, where thousands of people with disabilities were murdered. Tillmann, who headed the T4 administrative office, chaired the monthly meeting of local T4 office managers at various killing centers and on at least one occasion observed a mass gassing.[3]

SUPERVISORS

Christian Wirth has been described as "undoubtedly the most important nonmedical supervisor" involved in the T4 program. Although he had supervisory authority over all the T4 centers, he spent most of his time at Hartheim, where he served as chief of the office staff and director of personnel.[4] All sources state that Wirth was a cruel, brutal man who would do anything to ensure the "success" of the euthanasia program. He once shot and killed four female patients because their disabilities made it difficult to get them into the gas chamber.[5]

Like Wirth, Franz Stangl also worked at Hartheim, first as the head of security, and later, when Reichleitner succeeded Wirth, as Reichleitner's deputy. Stangl was later reassigned to Bernburg and in the spring of 1942 led a group of T4 staff members to the killing centers in the East where he served as commandant of Sobibor and, later, Treblinka. Jacob Woger served as supervisor of Grafeneck. Born in 1897, in 1933 he joined the Nazi party and the SS. By 1936 he had reached the rank of detective master sergeant in the Stuttgart Kripo, and in 1938 he was transferred to the staff of the inspector of the Sipo. After his service at Grafeneck, Woger returned to his old police job. Hermann Holzschuh was Woger's deputy at Grafeneck. Born in 1907, he joined the Nazi party and the SA in 1933, then switched from the SA to the SS in 1939. In 1940 he was recruited to the T4 program by Woger, then moved to Bernburg in February 1941 as chief registrar. After Hitler issued his stop order in 1941, Holzschuh left the T4 program for a position with the Sipo in Kiev. While less is known about the other supervisors, we do know that almost all of them had served as police officers and all were presumably members of the SS. The supervisors were responsible for record keeping, security, correspondence, registry, and personnel, making them deeply involved in all aspects of the killing process, from beginning to end.[6]

According to Friedlander, most of the T4 supervisors believed "that they were participants at the center of momentous events" and were "proud to be a part of the march of history." Friedlander cites Hans-Heinz Schutt, a supervisor at Grafeneck, as a representative example. In a letter to his stepbrother, Schutt exulted that they were living in "an age

. . . never previously experienced by a German." There is "only *one* victor," Schutt wrote, "and this victor will determine the future of Europe, even the entire world. And this victor is Adolf Hitler. . . . God's blessings, which accompanied the achievements of the Führer, have proved the truth of our ideology. . . . We enter a great, new Germany with the blessings of God but without the prayers of the priests."[7]

NURSES

Nurses also played a key role in both the T4 murder program and the children's killing program. After the war some nurses were tried along with the physicians they had assisted. Some nurses, had strong ideological motives for participating in the killings. But many others, like Anna Katschenka, had none at all. Despite her lack of ideological zeal, Katschenka helped murder hundreds of infants and children at a pediatric clinic in Vienna.[8]

Born in Austria in 1905, Katschenka attended nursing school for three years before working in the maternity ward of the Brigitta hospital, the infectious diseases ward of the Carolingian Children's Hospital, and an old-age home. She married a Jewish medical student in 1920, but one year later their marriage ended in divorce. Thereafter she suffered from mild depression and was sent for treatment to the psychiatrist Erwin Jekelius, to whom she formed a close attachment. In 1941 she began working at the children's hospital in Am Spiegelgrund, where Jekelius was the chief. Jekelius told her about the children's killing program and asked if she would be willing to administer lethal doses of medication to children with disabilities. She agreed, but later told interrogators that

Jekelius had first assured her that only absolutely "hopeless" children would be killed. After Jekelius was transferred to another hospital, she continued killing disabled children on the orders of Jekelius's successor, Ernst Illing. A postwar psychiatric evaluation found that Katschenka was intelligent and sane but concluded that she was highly impressionable and had greatly depended on Jekelius's approval.[9]

The nurses' reasons for participating in the killings were diverse. The following explanations were provided by nurses who worked at the Meseritz-Obrawalde hospital, where at least one thousand patients with disabilities were murdered during the Nazi era.

> Helene Wieczorek [accused of killing several hundred patients]: Director Grabowski told us we had to help the senior nurses—it was too much for them. We also would have to give the injections. First I refused and he said that there was no point in it because, being a civil servant of many years standing, I would perform my duty, especially in times of war. He added, it would be a law that the incurable mentally ill persons were to be released from their suffering. . . . I only did my duty and I did everything on order of my superiors. The Director Grabowski always warned us of the Gestapo. He said he would inform the Gestapo if we didn't do what he ordered.[10]

> Luise Erdmann [accused of helping to kill more than two hundred patients]: Through the behavior of Dr. Wernicke I realized that incurable patients were to be released by giving them Veronal or another medicine. I also declare that I, neither by Dr. Wernicke nor any other person at the

home, have been informed about the euthanasia. I wasn't sworn to secrecy in this respect . . . I was of the opinion that one took it for granted or believed that I would approve of euthanasia. My attitude to euthanasia was, should I become incurably ill—I don't make a difference between mental or physical illness—I would consider it as a release if a physician or, on direction of a physician, another person would give me a dose releasing me from everything. Despite my attitude to euthanasia, I have—when confronted with the problem—fought out serious inner conflicts. Euthanasia, in the form I experienced it at that time, after all was a killing of people and I asked myself if a legislator had the right at all to order or permit the killing of people. Never, however, did I hear about a corresponding law on the use of euthanasia but, on the other hand, Dr. Mootz explained to me once that there was no need for reservation as, should the situation arise, he would cover up for me. From this statement I concluded that there had to be a legality for euthanasia. . . . When I did participate in those killings and thus acted against my inner attitude and conviction, this happened because I was used to obey strictly the orders of the physicians. I was brought up and instructed to do so. As a nurse or orderly, you don't have the level of education of a physician and thus one can't evaluate if the order of the physician is right. The permanent process of obeying the order of a physician becomes second nature to the extent that one's own thinking is switched off. . . .

Anna G. [accused of killing 150 patients]: It is true that I was brought up as a Christian and that for my whole life I was convinced of the Christian faith. On the other hand, during my work, especially on the ward for the insane, I have seen such horrible misery and have seen all of the different sicknesses until the terminal stage. In view of these experiences, I have seen it as an act of mercy and a release when the killings were done. . . . I herewith declare that I have never been forced by anybody to participate.

Martha W. [accused of participating in the killing of 150 patients]: I've always disapproved of euthanasia. In the course of my work as a nurse, I could see that a lot of patients were sent to the mental institution who before had been very estimable people. It was a big injustice for me to kill those people because of their illness. When I'm reproached for the fact that I was brought up as a Catholic and the commandments also represent my convictions, this is correct. Until today, it is my conviction that people are not allowed to interfere. Nevertheless, I participated in the killings and I recognize that I acted against the commandments and my conviction and have burdened my conscience seriously. The only explanation I can give is that I didn't have enough time to think about it at that time because the nurses were put under a lot of stress.

Erna D.: Please believe me, that I didn't do it readily because I really detested it. I repeat, I didn't do it readily. In fact, I can't say why I didn't refuse.

Margarete T. [accused of killing 150 patients]: I was brought up as a Christian and still today I'm a very religious person and, as far as possible, I attend the service regularly. For this reason, when the killings began at Ward U1, I felt deeply guilty and still do today. . . . Due to the many years of working as a nurse, practically from since I was young, I was educated to strict obedience, and discipline and obedience were the supreme rules among the nurses. We all, including me, took the orders of the physicians, head nurses, and ward nurses as orders to be strictly obeyed and didn't or couldn't form our own opinion about the legality of these orders. . . . I was a civil servant at that time and, on one hand, I was sworn to secrecy and, on the other hand, I was obliged to obey given orders. I think at that time, I've always lived in conflict with my own opinion and the fact that I was a civil servant. On the one hand I saw the killing of people, even though it was incurable mentally handicapped people who exclusively were accommodated on Ward U1 as a big injustice and often asked myself why it was done. On the other hand, I was a civil servant and obliged to do my work and didn't see a possibility of getting around the orders. . . . You ask me if I had also committed a theft on order, I say that I wouldn't have done it. I saw, however, the act of giving medicine, even in order to kill mentally handicapped persons, as an obligation I wasn't allowed to refuse. In case of refusal, I always imagined my dismissal from the job of nurse and civil servant, which is why I didn't refuse.

Berta H. [accused of participating in the killing of thirty-five patients]: In other words, at that time I thought, I wouldn't be guilty if I didn't do the actual killings. To my own conscience, I always felt a little bit guilty and I tried to cope with it as far as possible to forget everything.

Martha Elisabeth G. [accused of killing twenty-eight patients]: Certainly I felt guilty about it at that time and, although I didn't do any killings by myself, I did help and I had a certain feeling of guilt. I'm only an ordinary nurse . . . and never realized that, legally speaking, I had become implicated in the killings. When I had to assist in the killings, I acted under duress and never with the intention to kill a person. . . . At that time, nobody would have helped us at Obrawalde if we had refused to do the work and there wasn't anybody to pour out one's heart to and who we could trust. As a sort of slaves we were completely at the mercy of the rulers and their political line.

Edith B.: Although I knew, respectively assumed from hearsay, that at Ward U2 (. . .) killings were done and the patients I moved to that ward possibly were condemned women, I didn't see anything wrong with it.

Gertrude F. [accused of killing five patients]: When I did it by preparing the medicine, I did it without any knowledge of legal consequences. The preparation of medicine in order to give it to the patient actually was one of my duties which was one of the reasons why I didn't realize that I did something wrong. I wasn't able to see a direct connection between my work and the killings. In addition you have to consider that I had worked in a mental institution for years and that the nurses were obliged to strictly obey their superiors, the senior nurses, the physicians and, last but not least, the director of the institution. In addition, I was the youngest nurse at our ward. Still today, I haven't completely become aware of my wrongdoing.[11]

THE CHEMISTS

Because the T4 program used poison gas to kill people with disabilities, managers relied heavily on the expertise of chemists, who were also useful because they could obtain those agents without arousing suspicion. Two chemists in particular—Albert Widmann and August Becker—played a crucial role in the T4 killings. Widmann was involved in the killings from the very beginning, including participating in early discussions about killing methods in the fall of 1939 and experimenting with gas and dynamite as a means of mass murder. Through his office he obtained gas and poisons for the T4 killing centers. He also secured the medicine needed for killing children in the pediatric killing wards and for some of the "wild" euthanasia killings. When interrogators asked him after the war how killing people with disabilities was related to the war effort, Widmann simply replied: "I never thought about that question. After [Arthur] Nebe told me that he had orders to kill the mental patients in his area, there was nothing for me to think about."[12]

After earning his doctorate in chemistry in 1933, August Becker remained in school for two years as a postgraduate assistant. He joined the Nazi party in 1930, the SS in 1931, and in 1935 joined the SS regiment "Germania" of the SS special purpose troops as staff sergeant. He stayed with the SS until late 1938, when he was assigned to work in the newly created Reich Security Main Office (RHSA). In December 1939, after a request from Brack, the RHSA loaned Becker to the T4 program so that he could provide technical support and share his expertise about the gassing process. He later described his work: "I functioned as an expert for gassing during the destruction of mental patients in hospitals and nursing homes." Becker frequently consulted with Widmann on procedure and attended the experimental gassing at Brandenburg. He also transported containers of carbon monoxide from the I.G. Farben factory in Ludwigshafen, to the various T4 killing centers. He later recalled that at the Brandenburg gassing experiment, Irmfried Eberl had opened the gas container too quickly, causing a loud, hissing sound. Becker showed Eberl and the others how to open the gas valve slowly and quietly so as not to frighten the patients. "Thereafter," Becker proudly announced, "the killing of the mental patients progressed without further incidents."[13]

BLOCKED BORDERS

Hoping to escape the mass slaughter of the Nazi regime's T4 and 14f13 programs, thousands of people with disabilities, like other targets of Nazi hatred, sought refuge in Switzerland. Their action was understandable: Switzerland had achieved almost legendary status as a neutral international haven. But this status was a myth.

After World War I, as a wave of xenophobia swept across Switzerland, there also developed an intense fear of people with disabilities whose ailments threatened to "weaken" the nation. Just as in Germany, racial hygiene soon became a standing, "self-evident" concept in Switzerland. For the Swiss, the "quality" of a human being in Darwinian terms was the sole criterion for a sound population policy. Under various cost-saving programs in different cantons during the 1920s, many Swiss citizens with disabilities were sent to

Germany for "treatment." Most never returned. Although we cannot be sure of their fate, it is logical to assume that most of them were murdered in the euthanasia centers.

In 1933 Swiss federal officials (*Eidgenossische Behorde*) created two separate categories of civilian refugees (*Zivil-fluchtlinge*). Political refugees (*politische Fluchtlinge*) were given blanket asylum, though only on a temporary basis. The admittance of all other refugees (*gewohnliche Fluchtlinge*) was restricted. Further concerns about a deluge of refugees (*uberfremdung*) and its deleterious effect on Switzerland's population led Swiss officials to prohibit all "undesirables" from entering the country. In 1938 the Swiss government urged German officials to stamp passports with a particular symbol that would indicate a person's background. As a result, an undetermined number of refugees were not allowed to cross the border and were returned to the Nazis. The numbers of people with disabilities turned back by the Swiss included both the 15 to 20 percent of the Jewish refugee population that was disabled, and those victims targeted directly by the Nazis because of their disabilities.[14]

Overseeing the refugee policy were the federal Bundesrat, which established policy, and the Grenzpolizei, which patrolled the streets and road border crossings. Between these two groups, extensive efforts were made to limit immigration, and restrictions were constantly tightened. At this time the Swiss added, for the first time in the nation's history, a mandatory visa requirement. Article 9 of the Federal Act of October 7, 1939, provided for the forcible expulsion of all victims of persecution who entered Switzerland illegally. Less than three years later, on August 13, 1942, the Bundesrat decreed that all individuals seeking entry into Switzerland without a valid visa would be summarily returned to their country of origin. Six months later, during the winter of 1942–1943, the Swiss frontiers were completely sealed off.[15]

Shortly thereafter, on March 12, 1943, the Swiss government increased its network of internment camps, which were used to detain refugees who had entered the country after August 1942 but who had not been repatriated. Many of the refugees who suffered from physical or mental disabilities were quarantined in hospitals and sanatoriums; others were put to work. For example, one refugee who was interned at Gyrenbad was forced into hard labor, fed minimal rations of food, and had to sleep on straw and dirt. He was later sent to work on an isolated farm. The fact that he had contracted polio and wore a brace on his severely deformed leg did not matter to Swiss officials.[16]

SWISS EUGENICS

As early as 1925 the Swiss Civil Code provided that "Persons who are of unsound mind are absolutely incapable of marrying." Despite one comment on the code noting that this law did not apply to "persons suffering from any form of insanity," it was in fact interpreted quite broadly. For example, under the code a person could be found fully competent to carry out a business transaction yet still be regarded as "mentally ill," thus barring him or her from marrying. But Swiss officials did not stop with restrictive marriage policies. They also intruded into the realm of human reproduction. Acting on the belief that people with disabilities were "unfit" to reproduce, the Vaud canton of Eastern Switzerland enacted a 1928 law that allowed for the compulsory sterilization of people with disabilities. This law, one of the first of its kind in the world, was noted and admired by Hitler, who requested from Vaud and the Bern government copies of laws that required or permitted the sterilization of "promiscuous idiots." Hitler greatly favored the Swiss law and used it as a basis for Nazi Germany's own sterilization policies.

The law restricting marriage, coupled with the Swiss disability sterilization policy, had a devastating impact on people with disabilities. Professor Hans Ulrich Jost of the University of Lausanne found that many patients with disabilities were victimized by the 1928 sterilization law, with females accounting for nine of every ten victims. But because sterilization was typically performed during another procedure, it is difficult to estimate exactly how many people with disabilities were forcibly sterilized in Switzerland.[17]

After the Atrocities

Between September 1939 and April 1945 the
defendants . . . unlawfully, willfully, and
knowingly committed crimes against humanity,
as defined by Article II of Control Council Law
No. 10, in that they were principals in, accessories
to, ordered, abetted, took a consenting part in,
and were connected with the plans and
enterprises involving the execution of the
so-called "euthanasia" program of the German
Reich, in the course of which the defendants
herein murdered hundreds of thousands of
human beings, including German civilians,
as well as civilians of other nations.

—Nuremberg Military Tribunal

THE WAR ENDED in May 1945 with Germany surrendering to the Allied forces. But the murder of people with disabilities did not end with the war, as evidenced by the
account that a German doctor gave U.S. Army representative Robert E. Abrams a full three months after the war.
This doctor had returned to his town, Kaufbeuren, after
serving in the war, and had observed psychiatrists at the local asylum murdering their patients. Abrams followed up on

this information and confirmed that the physicians in Kaufbeuren were still systematically exterminating their patients.
Indeed the American investigators who were sent to the
asylum found the bodies of several patients who had been
killed in the last seventy-two hours and had not yet been
cremated. They also discovered that over 25 percent of the
patients in the institution had been killed, either through an
injection of drugs or starvation, between August 1944 and
August 1945.[1]

American military officers also made a gruesome discovery in September 1945 when they investigated the hospital at
Eglfing-Haar. They found twenty children slowly dying in a
separate ward, the "starvation pavilion" used to murder children with disabilities. When the American officers arrived,
Hermann Pfannmüller, the director of the hospital, had already fled, but he left many of his files for his successor, Dr.
von Braunmuhl, to burn. But Dr. von Braunmuhl turned
them over to the American military government for use in
prosecuting Pfannmüller as a war criminal. Dr. von Braunmuhl told Major Alexander of the American military government that Pfannmüller "was a 'brutal fellow,' who enjoyed
killing his patients, whom he referred to as 'chunks of
meat.'" The evidence in Pfannmüller's files proved to be instrumental in reconstructing the institutional history and
policies of the Nazis' "euthanasia" programs.[2]

NUREMBERG

In 1946 the Allies—the United States, Great Britain, the Soviet Union, and France—held war crimes trials at the Palace

of Justice in Nuremberg. The first and most notorious trial was that of the major war criminals, including Minister of the Interior Wilhelm Frick and others. Subsequently twelve additional trials were held before the International Military Tribunal at Nuremberg. The first of these was *The United States of America v. Karl Brandt, et al*, also known as the Nuremberg Doctors' Case because twenty of the twenty-three defendants were physicians. Among the accused were Karl Brandt, Viktor Brack, and Philipp Bouhler.

The indictments contained four charges. The first was that the defendants had conspired to commit war crimes and crimes against humanity. War crimes were defined by Control Council Law No. 10, as agreed to by the commanding officers of the Allied occupying armies, as "atrocities or offenses against persons or property constituting violations of the laws or customs of war." Crimes against humanity were defined more broadly as "atrocities or offenses including but not limited to murder, extermination, enslavement, deportation, imprisonment, torture, rape or any inhumane acts committed against any civilian population or persecution on political, religious or racial grounds."

The second charge focused on the medical experiments the accused had performed on unwilling victims. This count consisted of twelve paragraphs, one of which described the killing of 112 individuals for the sole purpose of building a skeleton collection for a medical school.

The third charge delineated the defendants' specific crimes against humanity:

Between September 1939 and April 1945 the defendants . . . unlawfully, willfully, and knowingly committed crimes against humanity, as defined by Article II of Control Council Law No. 10, in that they were principals in, accessories to, ordered, abetted, took a consenting part in, and were connected with the plans and enterprises involving the execution of the so-called "euthanasia" program of the German Reich, in the course of which the defendants herein murdered hundreds of thousands of human beings, including German civilians, as well as civilians of other nations.[3]

Finally, the fourth charge named Karl Brandt, Viktor Brack, and eight of the other defendants as members of the SS, which had been "declared to be criminal by the International Military Tribunal in Case No. 1."[4]

In early October 1946 the opening statement for the prosecution was made by U.S. Brigadier General Telford Taylor, chief of counsel. Nine months later, on August 19, 1947, the tribunal handed down its judgment. Of the four defendants charged with war crimes and crimes against humanity, only one, Dr. Karl Bohme, was found not guilty. The remaining three defendants—Karl Brandt, Viktor Brack, and Philipp Bouhler—were found guilty and sentenced to death by hanging. After repeated appeals and requests for clemency, Brandt, Brack, and Bouhler were sent to their deaths on June 2, 1948.

Although these three men had to answer for their crimes, the overwhelming majority of the participants in the disability killing programs quietly escaped punishment. As Telford Taylor told the court, many of the Nazi doctors who committed the killings had either died or run away. Many of the thousands of rank-and-file doctors and nurses who escaped justice simply changed their names and resumed their

Karl Brandt, one of the two leading organizers of the "euthanasia" program. *(United States Holocaust Memorial Museum, courtesy of Hedwig Wachenheimer Epstein)*

practices as if nothing out of the ordinary had happened. Many refused to believe they had done anything wrong.

Of those few who were ultimately brought to trial, most were acquitted. Fourteen nurses were tried for mass murder for their role in killing patients at the Obrawalde-Meseritz state hospital, where between 1939 and 1945 more than eight thousand adults and children with disabilities were murdered. Most of the nurses defended themselves by claiming that they were simply following the orders of the attending physicians and were afraid they would be punished with dismissal if they disobeyed. All fourteen nurses in the case were acquitted. In another case, a psychiatrist who had not only killed his patients but had watched them die through a peephole in the gas chamber was also acquitted. And a court in Cologne acquitted a physician who said he had killed many of his patients because such creatures were just "burnt-out human husks."[5]

Why did so many perpetrators of these atrocities escape justice? As the author Hugh Gallagher explains, at the time it was exceedingly difficult to find doctors who were willing to testify against their colleagues. Authorities did try to track down and prosecute the more prominent Nazi physicians, but the results were disappointing due to the conspiracy of silence and denial that existed within the German medical community after 1945. As one doctor on the medical faculty at the University of Munster put it in 1951: what was the point of bringing up "the errors and confusion during the unfortunate period of National Socialism?"[6]

Of the thousands of individuals who willingly and actively participated in the Nazi regime's euthanasia programs, only a few were ultimately brought to justice. Their "punishments" were as follows:

Viktor Brack and Karl Brandt. Viktor Brack and Karl Brandt were among the 23 defendants who stood accused at the Nuremberg Medical Trial. For 133 days the Tribunal heard testimony from the defendants and 33 witnesses, including Friedrich Mennecke, who had already been sentenced to death for his role in Nazi atrocities, and Dr. Hermann Pfannmüller. But of all the testimony offered at trial, Brack's was the most revealing. After explaining the purpose and procedures of the T4 program, Brack tried to exculpate himself on lofty moral and philosophical grounds. "The life of the insane person has, for himself and for his relatives, lost all purpose and consists only of pain," Brack calmly explained. "Just as the soul belongs in the helping hands of a priest, so the body belongs in the helping hands of the physician. Only so can the sick person really be assisted. In that case . . . it is his [the doctor's] duty to free the person from his unworthy condition, so—I might even say—from his prison."[7]

Like Brack, Karl Brandt characterized his actions as humane. "I do not feel that I am incriminated," Brandt told his interrogator at Nuremberg.

> I am convinced that what I did in this connection I can bear responsibility for before my conscience. I was motivated by absolutely humane feelings. I never had any other intention. I never had any other belief than that those poor miserable creatures—that the painful lives of these creatures were to be shortened.[8]

As noted, Viktor Brack and Karl Brandt were sent to their deaths for their roles in the murder of hundreds of thousands of adults and children with disabilities.

Leonardo Conti. Leonardo Conti was state secretary of the Ministry of Interior and a loyal member of the SS in July 1939 when Hitler appointed him to direct the euthanasia program. Pursuant to the decree Hitler issued in October 1939, all hospitals and institutions throughout the Third Reich were required to report, on certain forms, all patients with mental and physical disabilities. Conti was in charge of reviewing those forms. He was also present at the first experimental mass gassing at Brandenburg in early 1940 and personally administered lethal injections to a small group of patients who, in his words, "died only slowly" and thus had to be injected a second time. Conti later committed suicide. Some suggest that he did so in order to avoid being brought to trial.

Werner Heyde. Werner Heyde joined the Nazi party in 1933 and later became an adviser to the Gestapo. By 1935 he had become an associate judge of the Court for the Elimination of Hereditary Disease, which dealt with sterilization cases. In January 1940 he joined Karl Brandt, Viktor Brack, and Leonardo Conti at the experimental mass gassing at Brandenburg. Shortly thereafter Heyde moved to Berlin to become a T4 medical director and to supervise a staff of approximately thirty physicians. In 1947 he was arrested by the Allies, but he escaped and eventually resumed his work as a psychiatrist under the alias of "Dr. Sawade." As Dr. Sawade, Heyde served as a psychiatric consultant in the courts of the Schleswig-Holstein district of Germany, even though the director of the Social Court, the chief justice of the provincial Social Court, two presidents of the Senate, and a federal judge all knew his true identity. Heyde was later rearrested but committed suicide in his cell in 1961 before being tried.[9]

Hans Hefelmann. Hans Hefelmann, a top KdF official, evaded arrest for twenty-five years. In January 1945 he began running a home for refugees in the former asylum of Stadtroda. After the Allies arrived, Hefelmann escaped to Munich, Innsbruck, and, later, Buenos Aires. During that time he worked as a driver for a cheese wholesaler, in a brewery, on construction sites, and managing a German-language bookshop in Argentina. He returned to the federal republic in 1955, where he lived undisturbed until the authorities began closing in on him. Hefelmann finally surrendered in 1960. His trial began in 1964, but his lawyers claimed that he was suffering from an unknown terminal illness, and the trial was suspended until October 1972, at which point Hefelmann was declared permanently unfit to stand trial.[10]

Ernst Rudin. In 1933, Ernst Rudin was promoted within the Third Reich to be commissioner of the German Society for Racial Hygiene and was named chairman of the Advisory Board of Experts on Population and Racial Politics. In addition to being the principal drafter of the Sterilization Law, he was also the co-author of a treatise cited by the Nazis as justification for the Law for the Prevention of Genetically Diseased Children.

It is difficult to overstate Rudin's influence on Nazi attitudes toward the disabled. In 1937 he joined the Nazi party and two years later was awarded the Goethe Medal for Art and Science by Adolf Hitler. Five years later Hitler personally honored Rudin with a bronze medal embossed with a swastika, bestowing on him the honorary title of "Pioneer of Racial Hygiene." In 1943 Rudin praised Hitler for his "decisive . . . path-breaking step toward making racial hygiene a fact among the German people . . . and inhibiting the propagation of the congenitally ill and inferior." He also praised the SS for "its ultimate goal, the creation of a special group of medically superior and healthy people of the German Nordic type."[11]

In November 1945, Rudin was removed from his directorship at the Kaiser Wilhelm Institute by the American military government, but he was never brought to trial. He is one of the many German physicians who played a major role in the extermination of Europe's disabled population but who escaped punishment, claiming all the while that he had done nothing wrong.

Paul Nitsche. Paul Nitsche, who replaced Werner Heyde as T4 medical director, played a central role in all phases of the euthanasia program. He was found guilty at Nuremberg and was sent to his death on March 25, 1948, in Dresden, Germany.

Max de Crinis. An Austrian, Max de Crinis practiced medicine in Germany and joined the Nazi party in 1931. He was considered "the most outspoken and influential Nazi" within German psychiatry and was a consultant at the highest level of the regime. Some say he provided Hitler with the wording for the original "euthanasia" decree. By 1936 de Crinis was active in the SS and its Race and Settlement Office. In 1941 he was appointed medical director of the Ministry of Education. He was also a committee member of the Kaiser Wilhelm Society (which became the Max Planck Institute, involved in psychiatric research) and was a director of the European League for Mental Hygiene. While being pursued by the authorities, de Crinis killed his family and then himself on May 1, 1945, by swallowing potassium cyanide.[12]

Irmfried Eberl. Irmfried Eberl served as a deputy assistant to Werner Heyde. He supervised the process of assigning false causes of death on the victims' death certificates and helped establish policies for maintaining the secrecy of the T4 killings. In addition to serving in the inner circle of T4 psychiatric "experts," Eberl was given special authority to visit various psychiatric institutions to encourage their participation in the killing programs.

At the age of 32, Eberl became commandant of Treblinka. Drawing upon his T4 experience, he was able to construct the gassing apparatus for killing inmates. He also helped arrange the transfer of Jewish patients to the killing center at Brandenburg. In August 1942 alone he ordered the murder of 215,000 Jews. He was also responsible for the deaths of at least 18,000 disabled patients during his 18-month tenure as a T4 official. Like so many other Nazi doctors, Irmfried Eberl escaped punishment.[13]

Carl Schneider. Dr. Carl Schneider, director of the University Clinic in Heidelberg, joined the Nazi party in 1932 and became a leader in the field of German psychiatry. Forced labor, compulsory sterilization, and mass murder were his methods of "helping" his disabled patients. During the 1930s and 1940s Schneider obtained large sums of money for a research institute where he conducted "scientific research" using brains harvested from adult and child victims of the euthanasia program. He also played a major role in the T4 killings. Schneider was executed after being found guilty at Nuremberg.[14]

Hans Heinze. Hans Heinze, a top T4 Nazi psychiatrist, headed the pediatric department of the killing center at the Leander Institute at Brandenburg-Görden. He gained prominence in the Reich Committee for the Scientific Registration of Hereditary and Inherent Sufferings, the front organization for the children's killing program. In 1931, while serving as a physician at the children's outpatient department at Leipzig, he collaborated with Paul Schroder on a book called *Child Personalities and Their Abnormalities.* Heinze was dedicated to defining, segregating, and exterminating certain classes of people, following the dictates of Nazi doctrine and the precepts of "racial hygiene psychiatry." By 1940 the Leander Institute at Brandenburg-Görden was functioning as a halfway house for T4 "transports." Some of the sanitarium's children were sent to the gas chambers at Brandenburg, after which their corpses were returned to the Institute for "psychiatric research." The Institute was also used as a training center for other physicians in charge of killing facilities and was referred to as the "Reich's Schooling Station."

In 1946 Heinze was tried and convicted by a Russian military tribunal, which sentenced him to seven years' hard labor. He served his term in various prisons until 1952, when he returned to Germany and became an assistant physician at a sanitarium near Munster in Westphalia. In 1962 a preliminary inquiry into Heinze's wartime activities began, but several medical opinions certified him as "mentally unfit" to be questioned and unable to understand the proceedings. In 1967 he was deemed unfit to stand trial.

When Heinze died nearly two decades later, his obituary read: "At the age of 87, the former director of our department for child and adolescent psychiatry died on February 4, 1983. . . . We shall honor his memory." The obituary was respectfully signed by the board of directors and the director of human resources of the Neiders state hospital of Lower Saxony, Wunstdorf. It made no mention of Heinze's participation in the mass slaughter of tens of thousands of Europeans with mental disabilities.[15]

Dr. Hermann Pfannmüller. Dr. Hermann Pfannmüller, director of the pediatrics department at Eglfing-Haar, joined the Nazi party in May 1933. Pfannmüller believed strongly in the Nazi concept of "life unworthy of life," and called for the extermination of all "useless eaters" who were a burden on the German economy. In 1939 Pfannmüller explained to a group of visiting psychology students that mercy killings were currently being conducted on approximately 25 infants and children who were being starved to death in a special "starvation house." In 1943 he established two more "starvation houses" for an adult population. Approximately 445 patients died while under his "care." In 1951 Pfannmüller was sentenced to 5 years in prison for his role in the disability killings. While serving his sentence, Pfannmüller received a letter from his wife, Theresa, who was incredulous that he was being punished for his "humane" work: "Yes, yes, it's humane all right that women and children are burned out of their homes, that thousands are freezing, that refugees have to live outside in the cold, but it's a crime against the state that someone like you put to sleep the sort of lumps of flesh that you had there in the asylum."[16]

Julius Hallervorden. Julius Hallervorden was a brain specialist who was chairman of the Special Pathology Section of the Kaiser Wilhelm Institute. He supported the autopsies of euthanized children for research purposes and dissected their brains himself. He also conducted research on six hundred brains of Jewish victims from the killing centers of the mentally ill. Hallervorden fled to Giessen after the war, then directed the Max Planck Institute for Brain Research in Frankfurt until 1957. The Institute finally admitted that the "historical material" stored in its basement was the human harvest of Nazi euthanasia. The "material" was eventually given a burial at a Munich cemetery in the 1990s. Julius Hallervorden escaped justice.[17]

Valentin Faltlhauser. Valentin Faltlhauser served three years in prison for his role in killing more than three hundred of his patients. At trial he described himself as a "supporter of euthanasia" but was careful to explain that he did not kill his patients for "reasons of utility." "For me," he simply explained, "the decisive motive was compassion."[18]

Friedrich Mennecke. Friedrich Mennecke was sentenced to death for his role in the murder of at least 2,500 people with disabilities at Eichberg. He died suddenly and unexpectedly in prison on January 28, 1947, a few days before his scheduled execution.[19]

Walter Schmidt. Walter Schmidt, Mennecke's successor at Eichberg, was sentenced to death for his role in the murder of at least seventy patients, but his sentence was commuted to life imprisonment with hard labor. Following a massive clemency campaign, Schmidt was released from prison in 1951 after serving only six years.[20]

Werner Villinger. From 1927 Villinger was a follower of Fritz Lenz, a leading advocate of the racial hygiene movement whose published works were credited with influencing Hitler. Between 1934 and 1938 Villinger was a member of Germany's Criminal-Biological Society, whose chairmen included Ernst Rüdin and Lenz. On May 1, 1937, while serving as an associate judge of the High Court for Genetic Health in Hamm and Breslau, Villinger joined the Nazi party. Records show that during his tenure, 2,675 notifications for sterilization were reported, 600 applications for sterilization were filed, and 460 sterilizations were performed. Villinger is listed in official Nazi records as a T4 consultant.

After the war Villinger became director of the psychiatric clinic at the University of Hamburg. He also served as president of the German Association for Adolescent Psychiatry from 1952 to 1961. The Hamburg medical faculty described Villinger as follows: "Above all, as the leading adolescent psychiatrist in the country, it has seldom been mentioned that Villinger is also one of the most active advocates for the application and broad-minded interpretation of the Sterilization Act, and as a consultant he contributed also to adult euthanasia." In 1953 he was awarded the "Cross of the Order of Merit" and later denied his activities as a T4 consultant. He was never brought to justice for his role in the sterilization and euthanasia programs.[21]

Dr. Werner Catel. During the Nazi era, Dr. Werner Catel served as director of the Leipzig pediatric clinic where the Knauer baby was murdered. Catel was later appointed chairman of a three-member commission that supervised the children's killing program. After the war he was appointed professor of pediatrics and director of the children's clinic at the University of Kiel. In 1949 a German court dismissed charges against him on the grounds that he had been a person of "goodwill" and was led by his superiors to believe that his murderous deeds were legal. Although he escaped legal punishment, the publicity surrounding his trial forced him to retire from his university position. He simply returned to his practice and continued writing. In 1963 he published a book entitled *Borderline Situations of Life* in which he set forth the case for euthanizing children with disabilities.[22]

UNMARKED GRAVES

Not only did most of the men and women involved in committing the euthanasia murders escape justice, but the atrocities committed against disabled people in Germany, Austria, Poland, the former Soviet Union, and other regions during the Nazi era have gone largely unrecognized and uncompensated. Because of neglect by historians, as well as the political powerlessness and economic deprivation of people with disabilities, no memorial center or museum specifically for survivors with disabilities exists anywhere in the world today. Without a memorial dedicated to people with disabilities, there are no reminders to the world of the horrors inflicted on people with disabilities during the Nazi era. Without these reminders, the specter of a recurrence of this nightmarish victimization remains.

Moreover, while there are thousands of Holocaust museums and memorials internationally, it is exceedingly rare for any of them to give more than a passing reference to people with disabilities. Most do not even mention the horrors inflicted on men and women with disabilities during the Holocaust. In Yad Vashem in Israel, among the acres of memorials and the tens of thousands of pages of text, there is only a single brief reference to the murder of people with disabilities.

After the war, disabled victims were not recognized as persons persecuted by the Nazi regime. Survivors received no restitution for time spent in the killing hospitals nor for their forced sterilization. Although the sterilization law had been declared invalid by the Allies, the postwar German state did not recognize sterilization under the Nazi era law as racial persecution, and postwar German courts held that compulsory

sterilization under the law had followed appropriate procedures. Men and women with disabilities who challenged such
rulings lost their cases in court when they could not prove that
the finding that had led to their sterilization had been "medically" wrong. Thus the appeal of a sterilized deaf person was
denied in 1950 after two court-appointed physicians certified
that the original finding of congenital deafness had been accurate. In 1964 the appeal for restitution from a sterilized person,
who during the Nazi period had been a student at the former
Israelite Institution for the Deaf in Berlin, was denied. The
postwar German court found that while the appellant as a Jew
belonged to a group recognized as persecuted under the restitution law, his sterilization as a deaf person did not constitute
Nazi persecution. To this day the German state has not fully
recognized and compensated people with disabilities, including the deaf, for their persecution during the Nazi period.[23]

One reparations court declared that disabled victims
were "people below the level of ciphers." Another court refused to punish those who acted in the euthanasia program
because euthanasia had its supporters before the Nazi era,
therefore the act was not punishable as a specifically Nazi
crime. From time to time efforts were made to expand German law so as to provide for those who were victims of the
sterilization and euthanasia policies. All these efforts failed.[24]

This neglect continues today. For example, people with
disabilities were designated as one of five victim groups but
were ignored in the notice process of *In re: Holocaust Victim
Assets; Weisshaus, et al. v. Union Bank of Switzerland, et al.*
The notice in the Holocaust Victim Assets litigation may have
been the most expensive and extensive ever given. The notice
administrators anticipated spending $2.3 million on notice for

Jewish organizations alone. Another $500,000 was allocated to reach Romani organizations and media. In contrast, not one dollar was allocated for organizations serving people with disabilities. In addition, no provision whatsoever was made for Braille notice, audio notice, TTY, diskette, large type for the vision disabled, or accessible computer technology for people with disabilities. The plan also provided for contact with more than six thousand Jewish organizations worldwide and perhaps as many as five hundred Romani organizations. But no disability organizations were ever consulted or informed about the planned notification procedures.[25]

THE PERSISTENCE OF
NEGATIVE ATTITUDES AND STEREOTYPES

Discrimination against people with disabilities did not begin with the Holocaust. Nor did it end with the defeat of the Nazis. On the contrary, people with disabilities throughout the world continue to be the subject of many of the same myths, dehumanizing stereotypes, and falsehoods that made their sterilization, exploitation, and extermination possible during the Nazi era. As Hugh Gallagher notes: "The Germans are not 'different' from Americans in any critical sense. . . . How they treated their insane, handicapped and retarded during the Third Reich was certainly extreme behavior—tragic and appalling—but it was not inconsistent with patterns of social behavior that can be traced throughout the history of the disabled over the centuries." And, "in fact, there is no reason to believe that the attitudes of the Germans in the 1930s toward the disabled and chronically ill were different in any essential way from the prevailing attitudes elsewhere."[26] Gallagher notes that there are many different clusters of attitudes and misperceptions about the disabled, some of which follow.

Blaming the Victim. The notion of blaming those who are chronically ill or disabled for their condition is, according to Gallagher, "caused by the degree of subconscious fear that the disabled arouse in the minds of most people." This theory was perhaps best expressed by the German Freudian H. Meng, who, in 1938, argued that "the nondisabled have a subconscious fear that the disabled person has perpetrated some evil act . . . that has brought on [his or her disability as] punishment."[27] In the Old Testament, for example, chronic illness and disability are called sins against God and his commandments. As Gallagher notes:

> The disabled is a sinner and,—as spelled out in Leviticus 21:18—he is unclean and thus may not be a priest, or even approach the altar. Twelve specific conditions are proscribed including "a blind man, or a lame, or he that hath a flat nose, or anything superfluous, or a man that is broken-footed, or broken handed or crookbackt, or a dwarf or that hath a blemish in his eye, or be scurvy, or scabbed, or hath his bones broken."

As time went on, additional deformities and illnesses were added to the twelve listed in Leviticus so that the later Talmudic scholars list 142 varieties of disqualifying conditions.[28]

The medical historian Henry Sigerist describes four different views of people with disabilities: The ancient Greeks saw disability as a facet of social status, so people with disabilities were treated as social inferiors. In Greece or Rome infants born with even minor disabilities, such as a club foot or extra fingers, were often taken by their parents to some remote place and left there to die alone. The Christians viewed the disabled as "objects of either pity or prayer." The ancient Hebrews believed that disability was caused by sin. Finally, the world of science regards disability clinically, as a symptom of disease, treating people with disabilities as patients in need of treatment and cure.[29]

Despite these varying attitudes and approaches toward disability, one thing remains constant: the tendency to blame the person for his condition. This tendency persists today.

Spread and Devaluation. While discussing attitudes toward disability, Gallagher explains two important terms: spread and devaluation. Spread is "the phenomena which occurs when some or all attributes of a person's character are thought to be a function of his or her disability." For example: "George has cerebral palsy; his hands move in a jerky manner; therefore he must be a jerky thinker, too." Another example is a paraplegic who happens to be a good student. His mental strength is often explained in terms of his disability: "He is a good student because he cannot run and play like the other students. All he can do is sit and study." German physicians were using spread when they assumed that because a person had some sort of disability, his life was worthless and meaningless.[30]

Similarly, devaluation is the "depreciation of a person's worth on the basis of his or her disability." Consider, for example, the Jerry Lewis telethons, which traditionally devalued the very people they tried to help. Jerry Lewis or Ed

McMahon talked about the tragic and pathetic condition of the many children with muscular dystrophy that they showed during the telethon. According to Gallagher, "their theory was: the more pathetic the victim, the more money would be contributed. In the process the child was [degraded and] devalued into a 'victim' and object." Of course the Jerry Lewis approach reflects an attitude that is both widespread in contemporary societies and has been prevalent throughout history. The "charitable model" (which combines pity for people who have disabilities with a moral imperative to "help" them) is often well intended but necessarily degrades and ultimately dehumanizes the intended beneficiaries.[31]

The Nazi German propaganda including such phrases as "lives unworthy of life," "useless eaters," and "human husks" to describe institutionalized patients is an extreme example of devaluation, as was the Nazi practice of referring to the people with mental and physical disabilities as *untermenschen*, or subhuman.[32]

The wrongs inflicted on people with disabilities are all the more remarkable because while they constitute a shamefully neglected minority in most countries of the world, they also form a very large group. An estimated minimum of 16 percent of any national population has one or more disabilities, and in many countries the disability rate exceeds 20 percent. People with disabilities nevertheless still face dire conditions of life, ranging from massive unemployment to near prison-like confinement. They are also often abused and neglected. Consequently they must continue to campaign for the most basic human rights and dignities.

This remains true in contemporary German society, where many people with disabilities are treated as second-class citizens and are viewed as economic burdens and inconveniences. Discriminatory attitudes have resulted in acts of targeted violence, including public taunts, insults, harassment, attacks, beatings, and killings. Neo-Nazis ("skinheads") have led this abuse. Reports show that skinheads have beaten a blind man to death, severely beaten five deaf boys, thrown a wheelchair-using man down subway stairs, and shouted taunts such as, "They must have forgotten you in Dachau," and "Under Hitler, you would have been gassed." The *Journal of the British Council of Organizations of Disabled People* reports that as many as one thousand disabled German citizens have been physically or verbally harassed in a single year. In addition, German police do not always document hate crimes or enforce laws that ensure provision of employment for people with disabilities. As a result of this discrimination, some people with disabilities are hesitant to leave their homes.[33]

Such harmful attitudes and treatment are not limited to Germany. Worldwide, people with disabilities continue to be marginalized and at risk. They face formidable and multiple societal and attitudinal barriers. For example, throughout Central and Eastern Europe, where many of the Nazi atrocities occurred, mass transit is inaccessible to the mobility impaired, and para-transit or alternative transportation is almost nonexistent. Accommodations are notable for their rarity in helping blind or deaf men and women. Braille elevator buttons or audio crosswalk signals are installed only sporadically. In Eastern Europe it is estimated that at least 20 percent of people who need wheelchairs do not have them. Most of those lucky enough to have wheelchairs find them costly, inadequate, inappropriate (being far too heavy, for instance), and difficult to repair.[34]

In short, the programs implemented by the Nazis to victimize and exploit people with disabilities were part of a pervasive and lasting legacy of discrimination toward people with disabilities. The rise to power in some European countries in recent years of ultra-right and nationalistic parties (which tend to view anyone "different" with hostility) adds to concern for the future. The Holocaust for people with disabilities must be viewed in a larger context that links memory, present realities, and future solutions.

SIX

The Need to Remember

THE HOLOCAUST was an overwhelmingly evil and moral catastrophe that remains a summons to memory. The wrongs inflicted during the Holocaust were not merely physical and financial; they were an effort to erase a class of human beings. People with disabilities during the Holocaust who suffered sterilization, forever shamed, and those exterminated, forever silenced, must be recognized and remembered. The Holocaust, which is part of the shared history of people with disabilities, acts as a warning both to the disability community and to all who care about liberty, justice, and fairness. It demonstrates in the most chilling terms the ethical, moral, and social failures that inevitably result when nations, societies, communities, and neighborhoods fail to recognize and nurture the humanity that is present in all human beings.

People with disabilities hold the same desires and dreams as everyone else: they hope for a good education, a chance to work, and an opportunity to take part in the lives of their communities. They want to be, and often are, parents, artists, professionals, consumers, teachers, business people, and taxpayers. The most formidable barriers they face, both physical and attitudinal, stem not from any individual disability but from arbitrary societal constructs that must be changed to accommodate the full spectrum of human abilities. It is, after all, in society's best interests to promote the full development and participation of people with disabilities, who can contribute in every area of contemporary life. A nation that neglects or rejects such a resource does so at its peril. With estimates from the United Nations that 25 percent of all the families in the world are affected by disability, public policies that ignore or marginalize a group so large and diverse cannot be considered enlightened or sound.

Finally, the suffering of the disability community must never be excluded or minimized in telling the story of the Holocaust. As Jewish people have long recognized, the key to "Never Again" is never forgetting. As long as history fails to recognize the persecution of people with disabilities, we cannot be assured that it will not be repeated. Indeed, it is worth remembering the words of Jean Baudrillard: "Forgetting the extermination is part of the extermination itself." Nor does it diminish the agonies of the other countless victims of the Holocaust to fully recognize the horrors committed against men, women, and children with disabilities. There is enough grief to go around.

The conditions that made the Nazi regime's murderous programs possible in Germany more than a half-century ago—apathy when confronted with affronts on human dignity, the presence of a charismatic leader who devalues and dehumanizes anyone different, negative attitudes and stereotypes about people with disabilities, and the manipulation of science and technology to achieve seemingly unthinkable goals—persist today in many parts of the world. We thus cannot assume that the atrocities the Nazis committed against the disability community were a unique event, never to be repeated. Our own self-interest, as well as our human obligation, requires us to continue to explore and remember these events and the conditions in which they occurred.

Notes

Introduction

1. Henry Friedlander, *The Origins of Nazi Genocide: From Euthanasia to the Final Solution* (Chapel Hill, 1995).

2. Michael Burleigh, *Death and Deliverance: "Euthanasia in Germany, 1900–1945* (Cambridge, Mass., 1994).

Chapter 1. The Children's Killing Program

1. There are conflicting reports about the Knauer baby's physical condition. See Friedlander, pp. 39–40. See also Burleigh, pp. 92–96; Hugh Gallagher, *By Trust Betrayed: Patients, Physicians, and the License to Kill in the Third Reich* (Arlington, Va.: 1995), pp. 95–96.

2. Quoted in Robert Lifton, *The Nazi Doctors: Medical Killing and the Psychology of Genocide* (New York, 1986) p. 51.

3. Testimony of War Criminals, *United States v. Karl Brandt, et al.* Quoted in Burleigh, pp. 94–96.

4. Ibid.

5. Brandt continued: "About petitions which he [Hitler] himself had received, and he told me to contact [Reichsleiter] Bouhler himself about the matter. I did so by telephone on the same day, and I then informed Hitler about my conversation with Bouhler. . . . But this was not the cause of the Euthanasia Program being started. In his book, *Mein Kampf*, Hitler had already referred to it in certain chapters, and the 'Law for the Prevention of the Birth of Children Suffering from Hereditary Diseases' is proof that Hitler

had definitely concerned himself with such problems earlier." Quoted in Burleigh, p. 97.

6. Ibid., pp. 98–99.

7. Ibid., p. 99.

8. Friedlander, pp. 44–46.

9. Burleigh, p. 101.

10. Table 1 is from Friedlander.

11. Gallagher, pp. 109–110.

12. A similar letter can be found in Burleigh, p. 151.

13. Quoted in Burleigh, pp. 126–127.

14. Burleigh, p. 103.

15. Quoted in Friedlander, p. 50.

16. Dr. Pfannmüller also killed many children by lethal injection of medication. He later tried to justify his crimes by explaining that "putting children to sleep was the cleanest form of euthanasia. . . . The child simply dies of a certain congestion in the lungs, it does not die of poisoning." See Friedlander, p. 54.

17. Quoted in Burleigh, p. 103.

18. Friedlander, pp. 56–59.

19. Ibid.

20. The term *treatment* was used because the phrase *to kill* was too incriminating to be used even in classified documents. After the war a T4 official testified about the authorizations: "Berlin sent us so-called 'authorizing' documents and these children, after a little while, would arrive too. . . . The children were assisted in dying." Friedlander, p. 57.

21. Physicians typically received bonuses of 250 reichsmarks for their participation in the killings.

22. Friedlander, p. 170.

23. Sally M. Rogow, "Hitler's Unwanted Children: Children with Disabilities, Orphans, Juvenile Delinquents and Non-Conformist Young People in Germany," Nizkor Project, Shofar FTP Archive File (http://www.nizkor.org), 1998.

24. Quoted in James M. Glass, *Life Unworthy of Life: Racial Phobia and Mass Murder in Hitler's Germany* (New York, 1997), p. 62.

Chapter 2. The T4 Adult Euthanasia Program

1. The German government's definition of euthanasia was expansive. It applied to all persons with a wide range of mental and physical disabilities, such as blindness, deafness, retardation, epilepsy, autism, depression, bipolar disorder, mobility disabilities, and many kinds of physical deformities, from harelips to missing limbs.

2. Quoted in Burleigh, p. 112.

3. Ibid.

4. Scholars estimate that in the official euthanasia program in Germany, at least 275,000 were killed solely because of their disability. But most of these estimates do not include (a) those who were gassed or shot when they became disabled due to botched sterilization procedures, medical experimentation, or maltreatment in concentration camps; (b) those victims who were both Jewish and disabled; (c) those with disabilities killed in occupied countries; and (d) those killed after Hitler put a halt to the official euthanasia program in August 1941. Taking these factors into account, it is reasonable to conclude that as many as 1 million people with disabilities perished during the Nazi regime. See Hugh Gregory Gallagher, *Black Bird Fly Away: Disabled in an Able-Bodied World* (Arlington, Va., 1998), p. 225; John Weiss, *Ideology of Death: Why the Holocaust Happened in Germany* (Chicago, 1996), p. 335.

5. The core group of medical professionals that initially assembled included Professors Maximian de Crinis of Berlin, Carl Schneider of Heidelberg, Berthold Kihn of Jena, and Werner Heyde of Wurzburg. Also included in the group were Dr. Werner Catel, Dr. Hans Heinze, Dr. Hermann Pfannmüller, Dr. Ernst Wenzler and Dr. Paul Nitsche, director of the Sonnenstein asylum. See Burleigh, p. 113.

6. Friedlander, pp. 88–90.

7. Friedlander, pp. 73–76.

8. Friedlander, p. 76.

9. Friedlander, pp. 83–84.

10. Friedlander, p. 85.

11. Letter from Dr. Wurm, of the Wurttemberg Evangelical Provincial Church, to Reich Minister of the Interior Dr. Frick, September 5, 1940, in *Nazi Conspiracy and Aggression* (Washington, D.C., 1946), Supp. A, p. 1223.

12. Ibid.

13. Ibid.

14. Letter from Reichsfuhrer-SS Himmler to SS-Oberfuhrer Brack, December 19, 1940, in *Trials of War Criminals Before the Nuremberg Military Tribunals* (Washington, D.C., 1949–1953), I, 856.

15. Friedlander, pp. 89–90.

16. Friedlander, p. 91.

17. Friedlander, p. 91.

18. Friedlander, pp. 96–97.

19. Friedlander, p. 91, 97.

20. Ibid.

21. Ibid.

22. Friedlander, p. 92.

23. Friedlander, pp. 110–111.

24. Friedlander, pp. 91–98.

25. Ibid.

26. Quoted in Burleigh, pp. 150–151.

27. Friedlander, p. 104.

28. Letter contained in Burleigh, pp. 151–152.

29. Friedlander, p. 92.

30. Friedlander, pp. 92–96. All these procedures were designed not only to make the killing process quick and efficient but to lull the patients into believing they were simply following normal hospital admission routines.

31. Ibid.

32. Gallagher, *By Trust Betrayed*, p. 12.

33. Lifton, *Nazi Doctors*, p. 101.

34. Ibid.

35. Quoted in Burleigh, p. 178. See also United States Holocaust Memorial Museum website, www.ushmm.org, Handicapped Victims of the Nazi Era, 1933–1945.

36. *Trials of War Criminals Before the Nuremberg Military Tribunals* (Washington, D.C., 1949–1953), I, 845–846. Burleigh, p. 179.

37. Friedlander, pp. 113–116.
38. Gallagher, *By Trust Betrayed*, p. 169.
39. Friedlander, p. 108.
40. Friedlander, p. 151.
41. Friedlander, pp. 141–142.
42. Ibid.
43. Friedlander, p. 142.
44. Friedlander, pp. 160–161.
45. Burleigh, p. 240.
46. Ibid.
47. Burleigh, pp. 241–242.
48. Burleigh, p. 242.
49. Burleigh, p. 130.
50. Burleigh, pp. 131–132.
51. The Einsatzgruppen was composed of six major units that were attached to the German armies after the invasion of the Soviet Union for the specific purpose of killing "hostile elements," including disabled men, women, children, and Jews. Organized by Reinhard Heydrich, the Einsatzgruppen consisted of members of the Secret Service of the SS as well as the German police and were subdivided into smaller units (Einsatzkommandos). Although mobilized during the Polish campaign of 1939, their main activity took place in 1941 and 1942. They were instrumental in killing hundreds of thousands of Russian and Ukrainian Jews and were the primary agent of the Final Solution before the establishment of the extermination camps. Often assisted by local police, the Einsatzgruppen gathered entire populations of fallen towns, shot them, and threw their bodies into large pits. They also used gas vans to kill prisoners and patients during transport. The Einsatzgruppen were disbanded in 1943, and efforts were made to conceal evidence of their work. The leaders were tried at Nuremberg, where twenty-two of twenty-four were sentenced to prison or death. From Walter Laqueur, ed., *The Holocaust Encyclopedia* (Yale University Press, 2001), p. 164.
52. Burleigh, p. 132.
53. Burleigh, pp. 132–133.
54. Friedlander, pp. 140–141.

55. Eugen Kogon, *The Theory and Practice of Hell: The Classic Account of the Nazi Concentration Camps Used as a Basis for the Nuremberg Investigations* (New York, 1998), pp. 35–36, 224.

56. Burleigh, pp. 220–221.

57. Friedlander, p. 149.

58. Ronit Fisher, "Medical Experiments," in Laqueur, pp. 1410–1411.

59. Leo Alexander, M.D., "Medical Science Under Dictatorship," *New England Journal of Medicine*, July 14, 1949, pp. 39–47.

60. Founded in 1939, Ravensbruck was a camp for women, though in April 1941 a small camp for men, technically a satellite camp of Sachsenhausen, was established nearby, through which approximately 20,000 inmates passed during the war. In 1942 Ravensbruck had 11,000 inmates. By 1944 the number had skyrocketed to 70,000. In all, more than 106,000 women, including girls and young women with disabilities, passed through the camp. Thousands died from overwork, overcrowding, squalor, and starvation. Many others were shot or gassed or died as a result of so-called medical experiments that involved surgery, amputation, and forced sterilization. Laqueur, p. 510.

61. Lifton, p. 273.

62. Quoted in Miklos Nyiszli, *I Was Doctor Mengele's Assistant: The Memoirs of an Auschwitz Physician* (1996), translated from the Polish by Witold Zbirohowski-Kosciam, p. 85.

63. Yehuda Koren, "Saved by the Devil," *Telegraph Magazine*, February 27, 1999, pp. 28–38.

64. Ibid., p. 33.

65. Ibid.

66. Ibid.

67. Laqueur, p. 412.

68. Friedlander, p. 131.

69. Quoted in Burleigh, p. 265.

70. Ibid.

71. Burleigh, pp. 265–266.

72. It is now impossible to know how many survivors with disabilities there are in the world who were subject to forced labor, except for the certainty that they constituted a significant percentage

of the general population. Disability Rights Advocates and its staff have been researching this subject worldwide for almost two years. But major data banks of Holocaust survivors, such as those maintained by Yad Vashem, the Simon Wiesenthal Center, and the Shoah Foundation, do not use disability as a research index. Records geared to disability are virtually nonexistent, and (as described previously) researchers have ignored the subject. Moreover, Hitler's forced disability sterilization program deprived an entire generation of heirs, and the perceived and internalized shame of sterilization has kept victims from coming forward. In addition, workers at some plants, such as I. G. Farben, had a life expectancy of only two to three months. See Weiss, p. 349.

73. Friedlander, p. 161.

74. Throughout Germany, in dozens of separate institutions, people with disabilities were routinely subjected to forced labor. "Judging from the annual reports of asylums, by the mid-1930s an overwhelming majority of patients were engaged in virtually unpaid labor, a fact that totally contradicted the repeated claim that healthy 'national comrades' were having to shoulder the burden of maintaining unproductive 'ballast existences' in so-called luxury asylums." Eugene Kogon, *Nazi Mass Murder: A Documentary History of the Use of Poison Gas* (New Haven, Conn., 1993), pp. 26–27.

75. More than 80 percent of the patients at Kaufbeuren-Irsee did some form of work in return for food, smoking materials, or small amounts of pocket money.

76. Michael Burleigh and Wolfgang Wipperman, *The Racial State: Germany, 1933–1945* (London, 1991), p. 247.

77. Burleigh, pp. 247–248, pp. 260–261. Disability Rights Advocates has also interviewed men and women with disabilities, still living, who were forced to work in factories under the Nazi regime.

78. From Disability Rights Advocates interview.

79. Gallagher, *By Trust Betrayed*. Current discussions of the need to "control costs" and to ration and prioritize health care based on economic rather than medical considerations (especially when accompanied by discussions of assisted suicide for the disabled) have a chilling resonance for people with disabilities today.

80. Friedlander, p. 173.

81. "Trusteeship Office East maintained branches in nearly all ghettos. Like other looted gold, what they collected was conveyed to Berlin, deposited at the Reichsbank, and melted down. Although precise figures are unavailable, most of it was shipped off to Switzerland. . . . Looted valuables were also consigned to safe-deposit boxes rented from . . . mostly Swiss, private banks." Jean Ziegler, *The Swiss, the Gold, and the Dead* (New York, 1998), p. 208.

82. From Adolf Dorner, ed., *Mathematik im Dienste der nationalpoliticschen Erziehung mit Anwendungbeispielen aus Volkswissenschaft, Gelandekunde und Naturwissenschaft* [Frankfurt am Main, 1935], p. 42. Quoted in Burleigh and Wipperman, *The Racial State*.

83. T4 internal statistical digest found at Schloss Hartheim in 1945. National Archives, Washington, D.C., T 1021, Heidelberger Dokumente, Roll 18, Item Nr. 100-12-463, Exhibit 39, p. 4. Contained in Burleigh and Wipperman, *The Racial State*.

84. Ibid.

85. Ibid.

86. Friedlander, p. 263.

87. Friedlander, p. 263.

88. Friedlander, p. 264.

89. Friedlander, p. 268.

90. Friedlander, p. 266.

91. Ibid., p. 270.

92. Friedlander, pp. 270–276.

93. Burleigh, pp. 269–270.

94. Friedlander, pp. 162–163.

Chapter 3. Racial Hygiene, Nazi Doctors, and the Sterilization Law

1. This section is based primarily on Robert Proctor, *Racial Hygiene: Medicine Under the Nazis* (Cambridge, Mass., 1988), pp. 22–28.

2. Ibid.

3. Ibid.

4. Proctor notes that, for American Social Darwinists, "economic competition was a natural form of social existence, one that would guarantee the success and prosperity of a society evolving gradually by variation and natural selection."

5. Ibid.

6. Laqueur, p. 508.

7. Proctor, pp. 22–26.

8. Ibid.

9. Ibid, p. 26–32.

10. Ibid.

11. Ibid.

12. Burleigh, pp. 15–18.

13. Ibid.

14. Ibid.

15. Ibid.

16. Quoted in Burleigh, p. 19.

17. Ibid.

18. Quoted in Proctor, pp. 40–41.

19. Ibid.

20. Table contained in Friedlander.

21. Ibid.

22. Quoted in Proctor, p. 69.

23. Ibid.

24. Ibid.

25. Ibid.

26. Ibid.

27. Proctor, pp. 74–80.

28. Ibid, p. 101.

29. Although the law was not intended to be punitive, many believed that the sterilization of "genetic defectives" might help eliminate crime. One prison cleric, for example, said that "when one reflects upon the fact that some proportion of the genetically ill are also morally defective and have broken the law, then one can easily understand how important sterilization may be in helping reduce criminality." Proctor, p. 102.

30. Table contained in Friedlander.
31. Ibid.
32. Ibid.
33. Ibid.
34. The proceedings of the genetic courts were secret. Even today most of their records are protected under German laws guaranteeing that certain data will remain confidential.
35. Friedlander, p. 29.
36. Horst Biesold, *Crying Hands: Eugenics and Deaf People in Nazi Germany* (Washington, D.C, 1999).
37. Biesold, pp. 36–41.
38. Biesold, pp. 42–43.
39. Biesold, pp. 45–46.
40. Ibid.
41. Biesold, p. 54.
42. Biesold, pp. 56–57.
43. Ibid.
44. Ibid.
45. Biesold, pp. 58–61.
46. Biesold, pp. 62–63.
47. Biesold, pp. 64–65.
48. Biesold, pp. 68–69.
49. Ibid.
50. Biesold, pp. 73–75.
51. Biesold, p. 76.
52. Biesold, p. 77.
53. Ibid.
54. Biesold, p. 80.
55. Biesold, pp. 144–147.
56. Ibid.
57. Ibid.
58. Ibid.
59. Ibid.
60. Biesold, p. 163, pp. 167–168.
61. Biesold, p. 168.
62. Ibid.

63. Biesold, pp. 167–170. Many German physicians did not participate in the Nazi regime's sterilization or euthanasia programs. Some simply refused to acknowledge the sterilization procedures, and there were a few scattered attempts to put together an organized resistance. But by and large, resistance by German physicians to both the sterilization and euthanasia programs was relatively scarce or at least rarely recorded. As we have seen in the euthanasia program, a physician practicing in Germany during the Nazi period could not help but know that patients with disabilities were being killed in large numbers across the country. Entire wards in hospitals were being emptied while once-crowded nursing homes and asylums were suddenly shut down. Indeed, the killing program became what Himmler had described as "a secret that is no longer one."

64. Biesold, p. 149–152.

Chapter 4. Perpetrators and Accomplices

1. See Friedlander, pp. 190–191.
2. Friedlander, pp. 192–193.
3. Friedlander, p. 194.
4. Friedlander, p. 203.
5. Ibid.
6. Friedlander, pp. 205–206.
7. Friedlander, p. 208.
8. Friedlander, p. 231.
9. Friedlander, p. 232.
10. Ebbinghaus, pp. 232–236, 243–245. Susan Benedict, "Nurses' Participation in the 'Euthanasia' Program of Nazi Germany." This report was the result of a fellowship for Research on Medical Ethics and the Holocaust granted to Susan Benedict by the Research Institute of the United States Holocaust Memorial Museum, with funds provided by the Merck Company Foundation.
11. All descriptions ibid.
12. Friedlander, pp. 209–210.

13. Friedlander, p. 210.

14. As Alfred Hasler explains: "No one knows the precise number of people turned away. No records of those refused entry were kept until August 13, 1942. Moreover, it is highly probable that the civil and military authorities destroyed many such lists after the war." Alfred Hasler, *Das Boot ist Voll: Die Schweiz und die Fluchtlinge, 1933–1945* (Zurich, Stuttgart, 1967). A published report by Christoph Graf, director of the Swiss Federal Archives, entitled "Die Schweiz und die fluchtlinge, 1933–1945" (Switzerland and the Refugees, 1933–1945), estimates that more than 100,000 refugees were turned back at the border. Ibid., pp. 208–209.

15. Only political refugees and military deserters remained exempt from Switzerland's restrictive immigration policy.

16. Hasler, pp. 21–24.

17. Ibid.

Chapter 5. After the Atrocities

1. Gallagher, *By Trust Betrayed*, pp. 206–207.

2. Gallagher, *By Trust Betrayed*, p. 207. Robert Conot, *Justice at Nuremberg*, (New York, 1983).

3. Trials of War Criminals before the Nuremberg Military Tribunals Under Control Council Law No. 10, Nuremberg, October 1946–April 1947 (Washington, D.C.), Article II, section 1, paragraph (b), I:XVI. Boerst 210.

4. Ibid.

5. Gallagher, *By Trust Betrayed*, p. 217.

6. Gallagher, *By Trust Betrayed*, p. 216.

7. Trials of War Criminals before the Nuremberg Military Tribunals Under Control Council Law No. 10, Nuremberg, October 1946–April 1947 (Washington, D.C.), Article II, section 1, paragraph (b), I:XVI. Boerst 210.

8. Trials of war criminals before the Nuremberg Military Tribunals, (Washington, D.C., 1949–1953), Vol. 1.

9. Karl Loren, "Psychiatrists: The Men Behind Hitler," Burbank, Calif.: www.oralchelation.net/data/psychiatry/data\8n.htm.

10. Ibid.

11. Ibid.

12. Ibid.

13. Ibid.

14. Ibid.

15. Ibid.

16. Ibid.

17. Ibid.

18. Ibid.

19. Ibid.

20. Ibid.

21. Ibid.

22. Gallagher, *By Trust Betrayed*, pp. 217–218.

23. Gallagher, *By Trust Betrayed*, p. 224.

24. Ibid.

25. Information gathered by Disability Rights Advocates.

26. Gallagher, *By Trust Betrayed*, p. 242.

27. Gallagher, *By Trust Betrayed*, p. 247.

28. Gallagher, *By Trust Betrayed*, p. 248.

29. Ibid.

30. Gallagher, *By Trust Betrayed*, pp. 254–255.

31. Ibid.

32. Ibid.

33. Diane B. Piastro, *Nazi Legacies: Hate for Disabled in Modern Germany* (New York, 1993).

34. Information gathered by Disability Rights Advocates.

Index

Abrams, Robert E., 143–144
Accounts: children's killing program, 27, 28, 33–34; scientific experiments, 77–79; T4 program, 31–32, 54–55, 64, 70–71, 88
Acquittals of perpetrators, 147–148, 153. *See also* Escape of perpetrators.
Ad hoc development of euthanasia program, 24
Administration. *See* Managers; National Socialist departments and organizations; Physicians; Staff
Adult killing programs. *See* Aktion 14f13; T4 program
Aktion 14f13, 17–18, 73–75, 93; mental handicaps, 74, 75
Aktion T. *See* T4 program
Alexander, Leo, 76
Allers, Dietrich, 128, 129
Allies, killing center discovery by, 92–93, 143–144
Am Spiegelgrund state hospital, 37–38, 131–132

Amputations as scientific experiments, 80
Anna G. (nurse), 133–134
Anthropology, racial hygiene and, 102–103
Archiv fur Rassen un Gesellschaftsbiologie (Lehmann), 99
Auschwitz: Aktion 14f13, 74; disabled boy (photograph), 29; dwarf experiments, 77–81; industrial forced labor, 85; prosthetic devices (photograph), 81; sterilization experiments, 76–77

Babies. *See* Children's killing program
Banks (Swiss): economic rewards of euthanasia program, 88–89, 176n. 81; reparations, 159–160
Baudrillard, Jean, 168
Bauer, Erwin, 104
Becker, Albert, 137–138
Becker, Hans-Joachim, 128

Bernburg State Hospital and
  Nursing Home, 62
Bertha H., 135
Bible, attitudes toward disabilities,
  61
Biesold, Horst, 110–112
Binding, Karl, 100
Birkenau, sterilization experiments,
  76–77
Blaming the victim, 9, 161–162
Blankenburg, Werner, 128
Boeter, Gustav, 107
Bohme, Karl, 146
Bohne, Gerhard, 128
Borderline Situations of Life
  (Catel), 157
Bormann, Martin, T4 program
  and, 41–42
Bouhler, Philipp, 16, 41–44, 74, 92,
  145, 146; photograph, *44*
Brack, Victor, 41–44, 75–76, 89,
  128, 145, 146, 148–149;
  Himmler's correspondence with,
  50–51; photograph, *43*
Brains: extraction for research,
  38–39, 52, 80–81, 153, 155–156.
  See also Organ sales.
Brandenburg, 51–52, 81, 153–154;
  killing methods, 51–52, 138
Brandt, Karl, 16, 22–24, 42, 67, 92,
  145, 146, 148–149, 169–170n. 5;
  photograph, *147*
Braune, Paul Gerhard, 67

Buchenwald, Aktion 14f13, 74
Burleigh, Michael, 82, 96

Career advancement through
  euthanasia programs, 128–129
Catel, Werner, 22–24, 105, 157
Charity as dehumanization,
  162–163
Chemical injections as a
  sterilization method, 76–77
Chemists involved in T4 program,
  127, 137–138
*Child Personalities and Their
  Abnormalities* (Heinze and
  Schroder), 153
Children: sterilization of, 112–126.
  See also Children's killing
  program.
"Children's killing centers" (table),
  27
Children's killing program: Allied
  discovery of, 144; death notices,
  28–31; deception by authorities,
  35, 170n. 20; development of,
  15–16, 21–32; Hadamar children's
  cemetery (photograph), *37*;
  killing centers, 26–28, 32–39;
  killing methods, 15, 32–34,
  38–39, 62, 170n. 16; legal issues,
  23, 34, 157; managers, 149;
  mental handicaps, 21–23, 27–28,
  36; numbers killed, 73, 93; nurse
  involvement, 131–132; parental

consent, 28–31, 34–35, 39; physician involvement, 24, 26–30, 32–39, 131–132, 153–155, 157, 179n. 63; registration, 15, 25–26, 34–35, 36, 149; scientific experiments by physicians, 38–39, 80–81; secrecy, 26–32, 35; SS killings, 73; starvation, 15, 32–34, 144, 155; table, 27; T4 program influenced by, 41–42; transportation of children, 26–28

Christianity. *See* Church

Church: Jewish patients in church institutions, 90; killing centers protested by, 49–51, 64–67. *See also* Religion.

Civilian refugees, 139

Clauberg, Claus, 76–77

Closing of killing centers due to resistance, 7, 51, 67

Community Foundation for the Care of Asylums, 45

Community Patients' Transport Service Ltd., 44–45

Compulsory sterilization, 106–108, 110, 112, 113–115, 119, 121–126, 140–141, 158–159

Comte, Joseph Arthur, 97

Concentration camps: Aktion 14f13, 17–18, 74–75; experiments on dwarfs, 77–81; forced labor for industries, 84–85, 175nn. 72, 77; killing centers compared to,

54–55, 84, 88–89, 153; scientific experiments, 75–82; sterilization experiments, 76–77. *See also concentration camps by name.*

Condolence letters: children's killing program, 28–30; T4 program, 49, 60–61. *See also* Death notices.

Consent: children's program, 28–31, 34–35, 39; cremation, 61; sterilization, 106–110, 112, 113–115, 118–119, 121; T4 program, 46–48

Conti, Leonardo, 41–43, 149–150

Crematoriums: celebrations of by staff, 63–64; children's program, 36–37; T4 program, 49, 51–52, 53, 58, 63–64

Crimes against humanity (defined), 145

Crying Hands: Eugenics and Deaf People in Nazi Germany (Biesold), 111

Cuba, sterilization laws, 107

Czechoslovakia (former), sterilization laws, 107

Dachau, 74

Darwin, Charles, 97

De Crinis, Max, 22–24, 43, 105, 152

Deaf people: community, 126; forced labor, 84–85; institutions for, 112–126; postwar disregard

Deaf people (*cont.*)
of, 159; as prisoners, 74;
sterilization, 19, 110–126, 159;
transfer to killing centers from
institutions, 123–125

Death notices: children's killing
program, 28–31; deaf students,
124–125; medical cover-ups,
58–61, 152; T4 program, 60–61.
See also Condolence letters.

Deaths: from sterilization, 76–77,
109, 123. *See also* Numbers killed.

"Deaths Resulting from
Sterilization Surgeries in
Germany" (table), 109

Deception by authorities:
children's program, 35, 170n. 20;
medical cover-ups, 17, 58–61,
152; Nuremberg trials, 89, 91;
pseudonyms, 30, 61, 146–147,
150; SS, 72; sterilization, 75–76;
T4 program, 17, 44–52, 58–61,
72, 75–76, 80, 83, 86. *See also*
Propaganda; Secrecy.

Denmark, sterilization for mental
patients, 107

Devaluation, 162–163

Development of euthanasia programs,
15–32, 41–42, 152, 169–170n. 5; ad
hoc development theory, 24

Disabilities as sin, 161

Discrimination. *See* Postwar
discrimination against disabled
people; Prejudice

District Instructional and
Vocational Institution for Deaf
Girls in Dilligen, 112, 118–119

Doctors. *See* Physicians

Documents: accounts of children's
killing program, 27, 28, 33–34;
accounts of scientific
experiments, 77–79; accounts of
sterilization, 77, 115–116, 121–123;
accounts of T4 program, 31–32,
54–55, 64, 70–71, 88; death
notices, 28–31, 60–61, 124–125;
Hippocrates' Oath, 95; Hitler's
mandates, 95–96; laws
sanctioning killing, 25, 42, 118;
letter on transfer of deaf student,
123; letters endorsing
sterilization, 113, 117–118, 121;
letters from physicians soliciting
organs, 52; letters protesting
killing centers, 49–50, 66; letters
on secrecy containment for
killing centers, 50–51; physician
evaluations, 45–46, 59, 120;
quotes of medical support for
programs, 25, 41, 96; records of
financial benefits of programs,
25, 88; records of Nuremberg
trials, 22–23, 143, 145–146;
records of personnel involved in
programs, 27, 104, 105; records
of sterilization, 109, 111; sermons
protesting killing centers, 65–66;
textbook math example of costs

for care of disabled people, 87–88

Dwarfs, experiments on, 77–81

Dynamite as a killing method, 68

Eberl, Irmfried, 51, 138, 152–153

Economic discrimination against disabled people, 10–11, 163–164

Economic justifications: euthanasia programs, 24, 25, 42, 70–71, 85–89, 101; euthanasia programs as wartime measures, 24, 42, 70–71, 85–89, 132; forced labor, 175n. 79. *See also* Economic rewards.

Economic rewards: career advancement, 128–129; euthanasia programs, 38–39, 52, 57–58, 85–89, 125, 170n. 21; forced labor programs, 83–84; industries, 84–85; plunder, 86, 87, 88, 176n. 81; starvation, 87; Swiss banks, 88–89, 159–160, 176n. 81. *See also* Economic justifications; Industries; Universities.

Edith B., 136

Education. *See* Institutes for the deaf; Propaganda; Universities

Eglfing-Haar clinic, 32–34, 71, 83–84, 91–92, 144, 154–155

Eichberg institution, 84, 156

Eimann, Kurt, 71–72

Einsatzgruppen, role in killing programs, 18, 73, 173n. 51

Elmendorf Remedial Training Institute, 123–125

Erdmann, Luise, 132–133

Erna D., 134

Escape of perpetrators, 146–147, 150–151, 152, 156, 158

Estonia, sterilization laws, 107

Ethical considerations: culpability of administrators and staff, 127–141; in medicine, 101, 131–136; moral benefits of sterilization, 177n. 29

Eugenics. *See* Racial hygiene movement

Evaluations by physicians, 45–46, 59, 120

Evolutionary theory, 97–98

Exhaust fumes as a killing method, 68

Eyerich (Dr.), 119–120

False testimony at Nuremberg, 89, 91

Faltlhauser, Valentin, 70, 156

Fedrid, Fred, 84

Feld-Rosman, Rose, 84–85

Finances. *See* Economic justifications; Economic rewards

Finland, sterilization laws, 107

Fischer, Eugen, 102–103, 104

Flossenburg, Aktion 14f13, 74

Forced labor, 174–175nn. 72, 74, 75; deaf prisoners, 84–85; economic justifications, 175n. 79; economic

Forced labor (*cont.*)
rewards, 83–84; for industries, 84–85, 175nn. 72, 77; Switzerland, 140; T4 program, 82–85, 174–175nn. 72, 74, 75

Forel, August, 106

Fraud. *See* Deception

Frick, Wilhelm, 83, 105–106, 145; correspondence to, 49–51

Friedlander, Henry, 51, 53, 58, 89, 91, 96, 109, 129, 130–131

Gallagher, Hugh, 85–86, 148, 160–163

Gamstader, Karl, 115

Gas as a killing method, 16, 48–49, 51–52, 53, 57, 62–63, 67, 72, 74, 78–79, 137–138, 149–150, 173n. 5

"German Doctors and Scientists Involved in Nazi Crimes: The Intellectual Mentors" (table), 104

"German Doctors and Scientists Involved in Nazi Crimes: The Medical Experts" (table), 105

Gertrude F., 136

Glassner, Leonard, 36

Gold fillings extracted from victims, 57–58, 176n. 81

Government. *See* Laws; National Socialist departments and organizations

Grabowski (Director of Meseritz-Obrawalde), 132

Grafeneck, 43–44, 48–51, 129, 130; killing methods, 48–49; public resistance, 49–51

Greece (ancient), attitudes toward disabilities, 161–162

Gross, Heinrich, 81

Guilt feelings of perpetrators, 34, 115–116, 132–136, 147, 149, 152, 155, 156, 157

Gunther, Hans, 104

Hadamar Institution, 36–37, 62–67; celebration of ten thousandth killing, 63–64; children's cemetery (photograph), 37; deaf students transferred to, 123–125; forced labor subcontracting by, 84; hospital ward (photograph), 63; resistance, 64–67, 84; starvation as a killing method, 71

Haeckel, Ernst, 98

Hallervorden, Julius, 38–39, 52, 105, 155–156

Harassment of disabled people (postwar), 164

Hartheim, 53–57; killing methods, 53; numbers killed, 93–94; photograph, 54

Haus, Friedrich, 128

Hefelmann, Hans, 128, 150–151

Heidebrede, 117–118

Heinze, Hans, 36, 105, 153–154

Hennecke, Gunther, 61

Heyde, Werner, 15, 105, 150, 152

Heydrich, Reinhard, 173n. 51

Himmler, Heinrich: Aktion 14f13, 74; T4 program secrecy containment and, 50–51, 67, 179n. 63

Hippocrates' Oath, 95

History: discrimination against disabled people, 161–162; Nazi racial policy, 9–11, 96–104, 106–108, 151. *See also* International community.

Hitler, Adolf: euthanasia orders by, 16, 17, 21, 22, 24, 42, 149, 152; physicians courted by, 103–104; racial hygiene and, 102, 103, 151, 169–170n. 5; on segregating the sick, 21; on sterilization, 95–96; T4 program, 41–42, 67, 92. *See also* National Socialist views on euthanasia.

Hoche, Alfred, 41, 100–101, 104

Hoffman, W., 114

Hogen (Dr.), 119

Holocaust, disabled people ignored as victims, 158–160, 167, 168, 174–175n. 72

Holzschuh, Hermann, 130

Homberg Institution, 112, 116

Hospitals: Inner Mission's Samaritan Foundation for Cripples, 43–44; Jewish patients, 90–92; Leipzig University

Children's Clinic, 22–24; Ursberg Home for Children with Mental Handicaps, 27–28. *See also* Killing centers; Scientific experiments; sterilization programs.

Hungary, sterilization laws, 107

Hunger houses. *See* Starvation

Iceland, sterilization laws, 107

Ideology. *See* History; National Socialist views on euthanasia; Racial hygiene movement; Racial policy; Scientific experiments; Universities

Idiocy. *See* Mental handicaps

I.G. Farben, 85, 175n. 72

Illing, Ernst, 132

Illness: as sin, 161; terminal illness laws, 25. *See also* Mental handicaps; Physical handicaps.

Industries, forced labor, 84–85, 175n. 72, 77

Injections: as a killing method, 15, 62, 80, 93, 132, 150, 170n. 16; as a sterilization method, 76–77

Inner Mission's Samaritan Foundation for Cripples, 43–44

Institute for the Deaf in Heidelberg, 112, 114–116

Institutes for the deaf: District Instructional and Vocational Institution for Deaf Girls in

Institutes for the deaf (*cont.*)
Dilligen, 112, 118–119; Elmendorf
Remedial Training Institute,
123–125; Homberg Institution,
112, 116; Institute for the Deaf at
Heidelberg, 112, 114–116; Pauline
Home, 112, 119–121; Schleswig
Institution for the Deaf, 112,
117–118; sterilization law
promoted by, 112–126; Training
Institute for Teachers of the
Deaf, 112–114; transfer to killing
centers from, 123–124
Intellectual attitudes and theories.
See History; International
community; Racial policy of
Nazi Germany; Scientific
experiments; Universities
International community: attitudes
and policy, 9–11, 19–20, 158–168;
sterilization laws, 107, 126,
140–141. *See also* Postwar
discrimination against disabled
people; Racial hygiene movement.
Internment camps in Switzerland,
140

Jacoby Hospital and Nursing
Home, 89
Jekelius, Erwin, 131–132
Jenne, Richard, 93
Jews with disabilities: experiments
on, 78–80; health care, 89–92;
killing centers for Jews with
disabilities, 89–92, 153; numbers
killed, 91, 153; refugee status,
139; reparations, 159–160
*Journal for the British Council of
Organizations of Disabled People*
report on violence, 164

Kaiser Wilhelm Institute for
Anthropology, Human Genetics,
and Eugenics, 102
Kaiser Wilhelm Institute for Brain
Research, 81, 155–156
Katschenka, Anna, 131–132
Kaufmann, Adolf Gustav, 51, 128
Kehere, Edwin, 106
Kiev Pathological Institute, 68–69
Kihn, Berthold, 105
Killing centers, 26–28, 32–39,
48–67; Allied discovery of, 92–93,
143–144; Am Spiegelgrund state
hospital, 37–38, 131–132;
Bernburg, 62; Brandenburg,
51–52, 53–154; children's
program, 26–28, 32–39; closing
of due to resistance, 7, 51, 67;
concentration camps compared
to, 54–55, 84, 88–89, 153;
conversion of hospitals to, 44,
129; crematoriums, 49, 51–52, 53,
58; deaf students transferred to,
123–125; Eglfing-Haar clinic,
32–34, 71, 83–84, 91–92, 144,

154–155; forced labor, 82–85; fraudulent expense charges to families, 86; Grafeneck, 43–44, 48–51, 129, 130; Hadamar, 36–37, 62–67, 71, 84, 123–125; Hartheim, 53–57; Jews with disabilities, 89–92, 153; Kiev Pathological Institute, 68–69; managers, 128–131, 148–157; Meseritz-Obrawalde Hospital, 82, 132–136; postwar killings, 143–144; public knowledge of, 17, 36–37, 49–51, 64, 66, 179n. 63; registration, 62, 149, 172n. 30; Sonnenstein, 57–62; staff attitudes, 55, 63–64, 88, 131–136, 149; Swiss patients sent to, 138–139; table, 27; T4 program, 48–67, 82; tours, 33–34. *See also* Killing methods; Resistance; Scientific experiments.

Killing methods: Brandenburg, 51–52, 138; chemist involvement, 127, 137–138; children's killing program, 32–34, 38–39, 62; dynamite, 68; exhaust fumes, 68; experiments, 55–57, 68–71, 138, 149–150; forced labor, 82–85; gas, 16, 48–49, 51–52, 53, 57, 62–63, 67, 72, 74, 78–79, 137–138, 149–150, 173n. 5; lethal injection, 15, 62, 80, 93, 132, 150, 170n. 16; shooting, 72, 73, 173n. 51; SS

methods, 71–73; starvation, 32–34, 69–71, 86–87, 144, 155; T4 program, 16, 48–49, 51–52, 53, 55–57, 67–73, 137–138; wild euthanasia, 17, 69, 73. *See also* Crematoriums; Scientific experiments.

Knauer baby, 21–24, 157
Kohl (Dr.), 23
Koren, Yehuda, 78

Lammers, Hans Heinrich, T4 program and, 41–42
Lange Commando, 72
Lange, Herbert, 72
Latvia, sterilization laws, 107
Law for the Prevention of Offspring with Hereditary Diseases, 75, 108–110; Lehmann's commentaries, 99; promotion by institutes for the deaf, 112–126; section 6, 118
Laws: mercy killing sanctioned by, 25; sterilization laws (international), 107, 126, 140–141; Swiss immigration laws, 139–140. *See also* Law for the Prevention of Offspring with Hereditary Diseases; Legal issues.
Legal issues, 23, 24–26; children's program, 23, 34, 157; discrimination against disabled

Legal issues (*cont.*)
victims, 19, 158–159; Nuremberg
war crimes definitions, 145;
reparations, 18–19, 158–160;
sterilization, 75, 99, 105–110,
140–141, 150, 158–159; Swiss
immigration laws, 139–140; T4
program, 42, 43, 133, 136. *See
also* Laws.

Lehmann, Gotthold, 112–114

Lehmann, Julius, 99–100

Lehner, Ludwig, killing center
testimony, 33–34

Leipzig University Children's
Clinic, 22–24

Lenz, Fritz, 104, 156

*L'Essai sur l'Inégalité des Races
Humaines* (Comte), 97

Lethal injection as a killing
method, 15, 62, 80, 93, 132, 150,
170n. 16

Letters: condolence letters, 28–30,
49, 60–61; physicians soliciting
organs, 52; protests to killing
centers, 49–50, 66; secrecy
containment for killing centers,
50–51; sterilization, 113, 117–118,
121

Lewis, Jerry, 162–163

Lichtenberg, Bernard, 67

Limburg (Bishop of), 66

Linden, Herbert, T4 program,
42–44

Lorent, Friedrich, 128

McMahon, Ed, 162–163

Managers of euthanasia programs,
127–129, 148–157. *See also*
Perpetrators; Staff; Supervisors of
T4 program; *managers by name.*

Margarete T., 134–135

Marriage: sterilization and, 115–116,
121–123, 125–126; Swiss
restrictions, 140–141

Martha W., 134

Mauthausen, Aktion 14f13, 74

Mauz, Friedrich, 105

Max Planck Institute for Brain
Research, 155–156

Memorials, lack of, 158

Men, sterilization, 75–76, 111,
114–115, 122

Meng, H., 161

Mengele, Josef, 77–80

Meningitis, as a medical cover-up
for death, 59

Mennecke, Friedrich, 148, 156

Mental handicaps: Aktion 14f13,
17–18, 74, 75; children's
program, 21–23, 27–28, 36,
38–39; Einsatzgruppen killings,
18; Ministry of Justice
Commission laws, 25;
propaganda on, 87–88, 96,
100–101; racialist policy
development, 96–104; scholarly
attitudes toward, 19–20, 39,

100–101, 104, 106–108; scientific experiments on patients, 38–39, 80–82; Soviet Union, 73; sterilization of mental patients, 106–108, 111; T4 program, 32, 42–43, 45–67, 71–73, 74, 75, 133–135, 137–138, 152–153; types singled out for killing, 16, 45–46, 74, 171n. 1; types singled out for sterilization (table), 111

Meseritz-Obrawalde Hospital, 82, 132–136

Midwives, children's killing program and, 26

Ministry of Justice Commission, 25

Money. *See* Economic justifications; Economic rewards

Mootz (Dr.), 133

Morel, Theo, memorandum on euthanasia, 24–25

Muller (Pastor), 119–120

Muscular dystrophy telethons, 162–163

National Socialist departments and organizations: National Socialist Physicians League, 103–104; Reich Association of Jews, 89–90; Reich Committee for the Scientific Registration of Severe Hereditary Ailments, 25–26, 34–35, 45; Reich Ministry of the Interior, 35, 42, 90; Reich

Ministry of Justice, 25, 66–67; Reich Office of the Detective Forces, 68; Reich Security Main Office, 137; Reich Working Party for Mental Asylums, 45; Special Registry Office, 59–60. *See also* Laws; National Socialist views on euthanasia; SD; SS.

National Socialist Physicians League, 103–104

National Socialist views on euthanasia, 21, 24–26, 33–34, 50; economic rewards, 38–39, 52, 57–58, 83–86, 125; history of racial policy, 96–104, 106–108, 151; Hitler edicts, 16, 17, 21, 22, 24, 42, 152; institutes for the deaf, 112–126; killing center staff, 55, 63–64, 88, 131–136, 149; official memoranda, 24–25; response to resistance to killing centers, 49–51, 64–67; scholarly positions, 39, 41, 100–101, 104, 106–108, 112–113, 153–154; supervisors, 130–131. *See also* Deception by authorities; Hitler; National Socialist departments and organizations; Propaganda; Racial policy of Nazi Germany; Secrecy.

Nebe, Arthur, 68, 137

Neuengamme, Aktion 14f13, 74

Nitsche, Paul, 80, 105, 152

Numbers killed: Aktion 14f13, 93; children's programs, 73, 93; Jewish patients with disabilities, 91, 153; Soviet Union, 73; sterilization surgeries, 109, 110, 156–157; T4 program, 6, 51, 57, 62, 67, 69, 73, 91, 93–94, 171n. 4; wild euthanasia, 17, 69, 73

Nuremberg trials, 144–157; acquittals, 147–148, 153; crimes definitions, 145–146; documents, 22–23, 143, 145–146; Einsatzgruppen leaders, 173n. 51; false testimony, 89, 91; Knauer baby, 22–24

Nurses: postwar, 146–147; role in euthanasia programs, 63, 88, 127, 131–136, 146–147. *See also* Physicians.

Obedience of perpetrators, 133, 135, 136, 137

Oels, Arbold, 128

Organ sales to research centers, 38–39, 52, 57. *See also* Brains.

Origin of Species (Darwin), 97

Ovitch, Perla, 78–80

Panse, Friedrich, 105

Parental consent: children's program, 28–31, 34–35, 39; sterilization of deaf students, 113–114, 118, 121

Parental resistance to children's killing program, 30–31, 35

Pauline Home, 112, 119–121

Permission for the Destruction of Life Unworthy of Life (Binding and Hoche), 100–101

Perpetrators, 127–141; children's program, 27; guilt feelings, 34, 57, 115–116, 132–136, 147, 149, 152, 155, 156; obedience as a factor, 133, 135, 136, 137; postwar escape, 146–147, 150–151, 152, 156, 158; sterilization program, 104–105; suicide of, 150, 152. *See also* Managers; Nuremberg trials; Nurses; Physicians; Staff; Supervisors; *perpetrators by name.*

Pfannmüller, Hermann, 32–34, 39, 71, 92, 144, 148, 154–155, 170n. 16

Pfingsten, Georg, 117

Physical handicaps: children's program, 38; disabled boy (photograph), 29; propaganda on, 100, 111; racialist policy development, 96–104, 112–113; types singled out for killing, 16, 38, 69, 74, 83, 171n. 1; types singled out for sterilization (table), 111. *See also* Deaf people; Mental handicaps.

Physicians: Allied forensic pathologists, 92–93; children's

killing program, 24, 26–30, 32–39, 131–132, 153–155, 157, 179n. 63; citizen attitudes toward, 67; ethical considerations, 101; euthanasia program contributors (tables), 27, 104, 105; evaluations, 45–46, 59, 120; Hippocrates' Oath, 95; medical cover-ups, 17, 58–61, 152; National Socialist Physicians League, 103–104; Nuremberg trials, 144–157; organ sales to research centers, 38–39, 52, 57; postwar reactions to euthanasia programs, 34, 39, 146–147, 148; pseudonyms used by, 30, 61, 146–147, 150; racial purity theories and, 102–104; resistance, 179n. 63; rewards for killings, 35–36, 38–39, 170n. 21; T4 program, 41, 42–44, 46, 58–61, 64, 89, 171n. 5, 179n. 63. *See also* killing centers; Nurses; Scientific experiments; sterilization programs; *physicians by name.*

Ploetz, Alfred, 98–99

Plunder, 86, 87, 88, 176n. 81

Pneumonia, as a medical cover-up for death, 59

Pohlisch, Kurt, 105

Poland, euthanasia programs for mental patients, 72–73

Political refugees, 139, 180n. 15

Postwar discrimination against disabled people, 9, 158–168; accessibility, 164–165; economic discrimination, 10–11, 163–164; harassment, 164; legal discrimination, 10–11, 158–159; public policy, 163–168; reparations, 18–19, 158–160, 168, 174–175n. 72; stereotyping, 160–165; violence, 164. *See also* International community.

Postwar events: Allied discovery of killing centers, 92–93, 143–144; escape of perpetrators, 146–147, 150–151, 152, 158; secrecy about euthanasia programs, 39, 148, 150, 154, 155–156, 157, 173n. 51; secrecy about sterilization, 178n. 34. *See also* Nuremberg trials; Postwar discrimination against disabled people.

Prejudice: international aspects of, 9–11, 160–165. *See also* Postwar discrimination against disabled people; Racial hygiene movement; Stereotypes of disabled people.

Proctor, Robert, 96–97, 98, 99, 102–103, 107–108

Propaganda: mental handicaps, 87–88, 96, 100–101; physical handicaps, 100, 111; racial hygiene, 99, 100–101, 111,

Propaganda (*cont.*)

112–113; scholarly endorsement of racial hygiene, 39, 41, 100–101, 112–113, 153–154. *See also* Deception by authorities; National Socialist views on euthanasia.

Prosthetic devices at Auschwitz (photograph), *81*

Protest. *See* Resistance

Pseudonyms used by medical staff, 30, 61, 146–147, 150

Psychological devastation of sterilization, 115–116, 121–123, 125–126

Public knowledge of euthanasia programs, 17, 36–37, 49–51, 64, 66, 179n. 63. *See also* Resistance.

Public notices of child deaths, 31. *See also* Death notices.

Public policy (postwar), 163–168

Racial Hygiene: Medicine Under the Nazis, (Proctor), 96–97, 98, 99, 102–103, 107–108

Racial hygiene movement, 98–101, 106–108, 112–113, 151, 156; international laws on sterilization, 107; Switzerland, 138–141. *See also* Racial policy of Nazi Germany.

Racial policy of Nazi Germany, 96–104; biomedical community and, 102–105; devaluation, 163;

modern Germany, 164; modern significance of, 9–11; propaganda, 99, 100–101, 111; scholarly endorsement, 39, 41, 100–101, 112–113, 153–154; Social Darwinism, 97–98; sterilization unrecognized as, 18–19, 158–159. *See also* National Socialist views on euthanasia; Racial hygiene movement.

Radiation as a sterilization method, 75–76

Ravensbruck, 174n. 60; Aktion 14f13, 74; scientific experiments, 76, 80

Records: financial benefits of programs, 25, 88; Nuremberg trials, 22–23, 143, 145–146; personnel involved in programs, 27, 104, 105; sterilization, 109, 111

Refugees to Switzerland, 139–140, 180nn. 14, 15

Registration, 149; children's program, 15, 25–26, 34–35, 36, 149; Jewish patients, 92; killing centers, 62, 172n. 30; newborns, 25–26; sterilization program, 106, 109–110, 116–118; T4 program, 16, 45–46, 92, 149, 171n. 1

Reich Committee for the Scientific Registration of Severe Hereditary Ailments, 25–26, 34–35, 45

Reich Ministry of the Interior, 35, 42, 90

Reich Ministry of Justice, 25, 66–67

Reich Office of the Detective Forces, 68

Reich, Otto, 108

Reich Security Main Office (RHSA), 137

Reich Working Party for Mental Asylums, 45

Reiter, Hans, 128

Religion: illness as sin, 161; killing center staff and, 134–135. *See also* Church.

Renno, Georg, 94

Reparations, 18–19, 158–160, 168, 174–175n. 72

Research. *See* Scientific experiments; Universities

Resistance: by the church, 49–51, 64–67; closing of killing centers due to, 7, 51, 67; parental resistance to children's killing program, 30–31, 35; physicians, 179n. 63; to Grafeneck killing center, 49–51; to Hadamar killing center, 64–67, 84; wartime measure justifications in answer to, 24, 42, 70–71, 85–86, 132. *See also* Public knowledge.

Rewards for physician killings, 35–36, 38–39, 170n. 21. *See also* Economic rewards.

RHSA (Reich Security Main Office), 137

RMdI. *See* Reich Ministry of the Interior

Rockefeller, John D., 98

Romanenko, Vladimir, 73

Ronigk, Oskar, 116

Rudin, Ernst, 96, 104, 106, 151–152, 156

Russia. *See* Soviet Union (former)

Sachsenhausen: Aktion 14f13, 74. *See also* Ravensbruck.

Sawade. *See* Heyde.

Schafer (SS-Brigadefuhrere), 71

Schlegelberger, 67

Schleswig Institution for the Deaf, 112, 117–118

Schmidt, Hans, 68

Schmidt, Walter, 156

Schmiedel, Fritz, 128

Schneider, Carl, 80–81, 105, 153

Schneider, Willy, 128

Schueppe, Wilhelm Gustav, 68–69

Schultz, Walter, 70–71

Schumann, Horst, sterilization experiments, 75–76

Schutt, Hans-Heinz, 130–131

Scientific experiments: amputations, 80; brains harvested for research, 38–39, 52, 80–81, 153, 155–156; children's programs, 38–39, 80–81;

Scientific experiments (*cont.*)
concentration camps, 75–82;
dwarfs, 77–81; ethical
considerations, 101; on Jews,
78–80; mass killing methods,
55–57, 68–71, 138, 149–150; mass
sterilization methods, 75–77;
mental patients, 38–39, 80–82;
Nuremberg trials, 145; racialist
history, 96–104, 106–108, 112–113;
university research centers,
38–39, 52, 53, 57, 80–81, 102, 154.
See also Scientists.

Scientists: chemists involved in T4
program, 127, 137–138. *See also*
Physicians; Scientific
experiments.

SD, role in killing programs, 73

Secrecy: children's killing program,
26–32, 35, 36–37; penalties for
breaking, 31–32; postwar, 39,
146–147, 148, 150, 154, 155–156,
157, 173n. 51, 178n. 34;
sterilization program, 178n. 34;
T4 program, 16–17, 31–32, 42,
44–51, 133, 152, 157. *See also*
Deception by authorities.

Sewing as forced labor, 84–85

Shooting as a killing method, 72,
73, 173n. 51

Siebert, Gerhard, 128

Siemens, 85

Sigerist, Henry, 161–162

Singer, Edwin, 114–116

Singer, Peter, 19–20

Skinheads, violence against
disabled people (postwar), 164

Slavery. *See* Forced labor

Social Darwinism, 97–98, 177n. 4

Sonnenstein Institution, 57–62;
killing methods, 57–58

Soviet Union (former): euthanasia
experiments, 68–69; killing
programs, 73; numbers killed, 73

Special Registry Office, 59–60

Spread, 162

SS: Nuremberg trials, 146, 149; role
in killing programs, 71–73, 130,
137–138, 149, 151, 173n. 51

Staff: institutes for the deaf,
112–126; killing centers, 55,
63–64, 88, 131–136, 149. *See also*
Managers; Perpetrators;
Supervisors of T4 program; *staff
members by name.*

Stangl, Franz, 54–55, 130

Starvation: adult killing programs,
69–71, 86–87; children's killing
program, 15, 32–34, 144, 155;
economic rewards, 87

Stauder, Alfons, 103–104

Steinhof children's wing, Am
Spiegelgrund state hospital,
37–38, 131–132

Stereotypes of disabled people, 10,
160–165; blaming the victim, 9,

161–162; historical roots, 161–162; spread and devaluation, 162–163

"Sterilization Applications and Decisions in Germany, 1934–1936" (table), 109

Sterilization programs, 18–19, 95–126; chemical injections, 76–77; children, 112–126; compulsory sterilization, 106–108, 110, 112, 113–115, 118, 119, 121–126, 140–141, 158–159; consent, 108–110, 113–114, 118–119, 121; deaf people, 110–126; deaths from, 76–77, 109, 123; deception by authorities, 75–76; experiments, 75–77; Hitler on, 95–96; laws, 75, 99, 107, 108–126, 140–141; legal issues, 75, 99, 105–110, 140–141, 150, 158–159; men, 75–76, 111, 114–115, 122; mental patients, 106–108; moral benefits, 177n. 29; numbers sterilized, 109, 110, 156; pain of procedure, 77, 121; physician evaluations, 120; postwar ignoring of, 158–159; psychological devastation of, 115–116, 121–123, 125–126; radiation, 75–76; registration, 106, 109–110, 116–118; secrecy surrounding, 178n. 34; tables, 109, 111; war's effect on, 123;

women, 76–77, 111, 113–114, 118–120, 121–123

"Sterilization Surgeries in Germany" (table), 109

Strokes, as a medical cover-up for death, 59

Suicides of perpetrators, 150, 152

Supervisors of T4 program, 129–131. *See also* Managers; Perpetrators; *supervisors by name.*

Survivors: forced labor survivors, 174–175n. 72; lack of recognition, 18–19, 158–160, 168, 174–175n. 72

Sweden, sterilization laws, 107

Switzerland: economic rewards of euthanasia programs, 85, 88–89; forced labor, 140; participation in German euthanasia programs, 138–139; racial hygiene laws, 107, 126, 140–141; as a refuge, 138–141, 180nn. 14, 15; sterilization, 107, 126, 140–141

Taylor, Telford, 146

Terminal illness laws, 25

Textbook math exercises, 87–88

T4 program, 41–94, 127–138; Aktion 14f13, 17–18, 73–75, 93; center of operations (photograph), 47; chemists, 127, 137–138; consent of guardians or relatives, 46–48; death notices,

T4 program (*cont.*)
60–61; deception by authorities, 17, 44–52, 58–61, 72, 75–76, 80, 83, 86, 89; documents, 88; economic rewards, 85–89; forced labor, 82–85, 174–175nn. 72, 74, 75; Jews with disabilities, 89–92, 153; killing centers, 48–67, 82; killing methods, 16, 48–49, 51–52, 53, 67–73, 137–138; legal issues, 42, 43, 133, 136; management, 127–138, 148–157; mental handicaps, 32, 42–43, 45–67, 71–73, 74, 133–135, 137–138, 152–153; numbers killed, 6, 51, 57, 62, 67, 69, 73, 91, 93–94, 171n. 4; nurse involvement, 131–136; physician involvement, 41, 42–44, 46, 58–61, 64, 171n. 5, 179n. 63; registration, 16, 45–46, 92, 149, 171n. 1; scientific experiments, 75–82; secrecy, 16–17, 31–32, 42, 44–51, 133, 152, 157; transportation, 44–45, 46, 72–73

Tiergartenstrasse 4 (photograph), 47

Tillmann, Friedrich, 128, 129

Tours, killing centers, 33–34

Training Institute for Teachers of the Deaf, 112–114

Transportation: children's killing program, 26–28; T4 program, 44–45, 46, 72–73

Treblinka, 55, 153

Turkey, sterilization laws, 107

United States: attitudes toward disabled people, 160; killing center investigation by, 93; racial hygiene movement in, 107, 108; Social Darwinism, 97–98, 177n. 4; sterilization laws, 107

Universities: Leipzig University Children's Clinic, 22–24, 80–81; racial hygiene theories endorsed by, 100–104; research centers, 38–39, 52, 57, 102, 153, 154. *See also* Institutes for the deaf; Scientific experiments.

Ursberg Home for Children with Mental Handicaps, 27–28

Villinger, Werner, 36, 56–157

Violence against disabled people (postwar), 164

Visas for Switzerland, 139–140

Volk and Rasse, 99

Von Braunmuhl (Dr.), 144

Von Galen, Clemens August Graf, 17, 64–66

Von Hegener, Richard, 128

Voneche, Jacques, 126

Vorberg, Reinhold, 128, 129

Wachsturmbann Eimann, 71–72

Wagner, Gerhard, 24

War: euthanasia programs as wartime measures, 24, 42, 70–71, 85–89, 132; sterilization programs greatly reduced by, 123

Wernicke (Dr.), 132–133

Widmann, Albert, 68, 137

Wieczorek, Helene, 132

Wild euthanasia, 17, 69, 73

Wirth, Christian, 31–32, 54–56, 129–130; photograph, 56

Woger, Jacob, 130

Women, sterilization, 76–77, 111, 113–114, 118–120, 121–123

Wurm (Bishop), 49–51

Yad Veshem memorial, 158

Yugoslavia, sterilization laws, 107

Ziereis, Franz, 94

Zucker, Konrad, 105

A NOTE ON THE AUTHOR

Suzanne Evans was born in Whittier, California, and studied at U.C.L.A., Western State University College of Law, and the University of California at Berkeley, where she is working towards a Ph.D. in U.S. history. Formerly a staff reporter for the *Los Angeles Business Journal*, her writings have also appeared in the *New York Times* and the *Wall Street Journal*. She has been a Fellow of the Smithsonian Institution and the Newberry Library, Chicago, and now lives with her daughter in Newport Beach, California.